# BRICKING
# It

## FROM STAY AT HOME MUM
## TO MILLIONS IN PROPERTY

# NICOLE BREMNER

# RETHINK PRESS

First published in Great Britain 2017 by Rethink
Press (www.rethinkpress.com)

# CONTENTS

# CONTENTS

# CONTENTS

# PREFACE

It's no secret that when I started out in property I knew nothing. Not a thing. Like many people, my first property development project was my own home. And that was it.

Now in my fifth year of property development, I have eleven projects on the go across London. These projects contain more than four hundred units and are worth over £120 million in gross development value.

In 2016, I received many invitations to speak at events and share my story. The question I was asked most often at these events was 'How did you scale up your business and portfolio so rapidly?' The second question was 'Are you going to teach people the process?' My answer is this: people don't need a teacher, they just need to get out there and do it.

This gave me an idea. If the best way for people to learn about property development is by doing it, what if I could let them see our projects as they are happening, in real time? Let them see everything – appraisal, acquisition, planning, construction, right through to sales – all the ups and downs of all our London developments?

And what if they could actually invest in one, or more, of my developments for as little as £500 and have a front-row seat to watch the progress of the development? That's when the idea of crowdfunding came about. I'm passionate about investors with smaller available funds having access to the types of deals that are usually only available to larger investors and developers. Crowdfunding has been incredibly successful, allowing my company to work with dozens of new investors and raise over £4 million in equity investment. And this is just the beginning.

At one of my speaking engagements a woman approached me and suggested that I should write a book. I told her I'd thought about writing about the property process to help others get started. She replied 'Boring – tell your story; that's what's interesting'. Of course, that planted the seed and by summer 2016 I had a rough outline of this book.

# PREFACE

This is not a book about how to get rich quick. I'm not selling the dream. I'm simply telling the story of how I scaled up my property business from my first property to a whole portfolio of projects.

I'm not going to give you all the answers. I simply hope that you can learn from my experiences and use some of the information in this book in your own property journey.

# INTRODUCTION

'How have the girls been?' my friend asked, as she picked up her daughters from a playdate at my house.

'Fine, fine,' I replied, noticing a flash of sympathy in my friend's eyes.

I knew why she looked at me with such pity. I was wearing saggy, stained yoga bottoms and my partner's old t-shirt, and my greasy hair was slicked back in a topknot – and not in the fashionable way. I hadn't stepped foot in the hairdressers in months, perhaps a year, and my face hadn't seen a scrap of make-up in weeks. Recently I'd even been out for a pub meal without make-up – something unfathomable pre-kids.

Kids changed so much more than just my body. The experience had also taken a toll on my confidence. Before kids, I'd enjoyed a moderately successful career in the City. After immigrating to London from Australia in 2000, I'd worked hard to be noticed for the potential I believed I had. But I felt the process was too slow and the promotions and recognition I craved didn't come fast enough.

I persisted until late 2006, when I decided that I was never going to get anywhere in the corporate world. I realised I had to be my own boss. My idea was Brittique, an online retailer for up-and-coming British designers. For twelve months, I worked tirelessly on what was essentially a flawed business model. In May 2007, my partner Michael was transferred to New York, and there was no way I could continue with a British-focused business in a different time zone. Then I found out, to my utter delight, that I was pregnant.

Having my first child was the happiest moment of my life. I enjoyed the tight-knit group of 'mom' friends I made in New York. They were educated women, mostly lawyers, who chose to leave work rather than take the mandated twelve weeks of maternity leave. That first summer spent in the pristine parks of a surprisingly green New York City was one of the best in my life.

Not the type to sit and play with the baby all day, after six months I needed more. I missed the stimulation of working and earning my own money. I took up a contract in the equity research department at Goldman Sachs on Wall Street.

Working on Wall Street was a dream come true. Especially in a firm like Goldman Sachs. I felt like I'd entered a private club and that I'd arrived at the pinnacle of my career. But my first day at work was 15 September 2008 – the day when Lehman Brothers collapsed, triggering the global financial crisis.

With the financial markets in turmoil, no one had time to integrate a new recruit. I spent a couple of months watching the events unfold on CNN and trying to make myself useful. It was hardly the fulfilment of my dream. As the markets crumbled, Michael told me we needed to move back to London because it was more stable. At the same time I discovered, once again to my delight, that I was expecting baby number two.

After my brief return to banking, it was clear to me that I could never go back to a corporate career. My small taste of entrepreneurship had whetted my appetite. I needed to be my own boss. Even though the corporate world was a fast-paced environment, it moved too slowly for me. With the financial world in turmoil, a second-tier analyst like me wouldn't be able to secure a top-rate job. It was time to look at other career options. But first, I had two babies to raise and a partner who worked eighteen hours a day, seven days a week. It took years – and plenty of trial and error – to find my true niche.

# Why Property?

As you're reading this book, you may already be sold on the idea of property as a career choice. It wasn't always obvious for me. In May 2011, I had our third child in three years and three months (what is it about three?) and I was lost. I had no idea what I wanted to do with my life. I knew I couldn't go back into banking, with the long hours and frequent travel. I tried photography (specifically food), blogging, cooking, knitting and crochet. These were all creative, but none of them allowed me to contribute to the family finances in the way I wanted to. It was such hard work for so little return.

Living in a beautifully renovated home with a large kitchen and seven ovens, cooking was the obvious choice. Cupcakes and mummy blogging were hot in the early 2010s, so I jumped on the bandwagon.

The cooking bit was a cinch. I'd cooked from the time I was young, with my grandma and with my mother. I was raised vegetarian and had recently given up all meat and dairy again, so being a vegan mummy blogger and photographer was a natural choice.

It was creative work and my family (mostly) didn't complain about the vast array of baked goods available. The neighbours didn't either; someone had to eat all those cakes. But getting any traffic to a blog was an uphill battle. Even after a phone call asking me to become a contestant on *The Great British Bake Off*, I knew I was never going to be able to contribute significantly to the family income. I also needed the intellectual stimulation I missed about banking.

I vented my frustrations to Michael, whose career was going from strength to strength. After hours of discussion, he suggested property. I'd never considered it as a career, but it was true that I knew the house prices of most properties for sale in my area of Hackney. I knew which properties needed work and what work was underway. I had enjoyed the process of renovating my home and I was still in touch with my builder. It seemed ideal.

The plan was to buy flats in Hackney for around £500,000, renovate them to look like the shabby-chic Pinterest flats I loved, and sell them to others who appreciated my style. It would keep me entertained and help me make a little money.

It was 2012 and the market in Hackney was hot. It had the fastest-growing house prices in the country, with growth of over 700% in 20 years[1]. As a newbie with £500,000 of cash savings, you'd think that agents would be falling all over me. But everyone, it seemed, was buying.

I'd attend auctions and be outbid significantly. People were making silly offers and throwing silly money around. I realised that if I wanted to compete with these developers I needed to go bigger. I needed £1 million.

I explained my issue to Michael and asked that we increase our purchasing budget. Incredibly, Michael agreed with my analysis and allowed me to use the fund from the sale of our Clerkenwell flat, plus some more, to buy my first investment property, Lenthall Road.

On a quiet road close to London Fields in Hackney, the property had been empty for the last eighteen months while eleven siblings battled out the will after the death of their

---

1 https://www.ft.com/content/40a55dce-f461-11e6-8758 -687615182116

father. Credit to the father, a former bus driver, he had bought each of his children a property in Hackney. There were just issues with one child claiming that his property wasn't worth as much as the others were.

Lenthall Road had already gone under offer at £1 million, but the potential buyer wasn't performing so the agent allowed me to gazump. (I know, I know – evil.) We knew that we would need to add a significant amount to move the vendors to accept our offer, so I went with £1.1 million and the vendors accepted.

As a cash buyer, I quickly put down a deposit and went through the conveyancing process without an issue. A couple of months later I was the owner of a shabby former house of multiple occupation (HMO) with questionable greenery growing in the garden (one of the builders was quick to clear it on his own time, much to the disappointment of a neighbour).

The reason property investment is such a good fit for me is that it offers me the three Fs:

Freedom: from the job, a boss, commuting, the nine-to-five.

Flexibility: to work as many hours as I want at the times

I want. Property works well for stay-at-home parents, who can work around school hours.

Financial independence: the ability to contribute to the family finances, being paid for the effort I put in.

As the main carer for the children and with a partner who worked long hours, I needed something that I could plan around the children and never have to feel that guilt of missing a school play or sporting event.

The best bit about a property career is that it allows me to contribute significantly to the family finances and feel like I am doing my bit. It's also creative and allows me to build homes that people aspire to live in; I'm proud of the level of detail and the quality of the homes we produce. I'm also doing a small bit to ease the housing shortage.

According to an article in the *Telegraph*[2], the Department for Communities and Local Government believes that more than five million new homes are needed over the next twenty-five years to cope with the growth in immigration and an ageing population. The increase in older single-person households will be the biggest contributor. According to Migration Watch UK, even after the Brexit vote, net immigration figures are

---

2 http://www.telegraph.co.uk/news/2016/07/12/53-million-new-ho mes-needed-as-ageing-and-immigration-drive-dema/

forecast at 170,000 a year. All these people need a home. Not all will buy, of course, but someone has to provide this housing and that might as well be you, right?

But, you may ask, won't I lose money in property? According to the Office for National Statistics average UK house price data[3], the largest drop in house prices happened between September 2007 and March 2009 when UK property prices fell by 19%. So, what's all this talk about huge drops and developers being wiped out? Obviously, some areas were impacted more than others and parts of the UK still have not recovered their pre-2008 levels. Today, however, UK house prices on average are over 41% higher than their 2009 lows.

If you want to understand more about house prices, I'd recommend you read an excellent article by Tom Ough in the *Telegraph* entitled, 'The state of the UK housing market in five charts'[4].

At the risk of being London-centric, I'd like to look at London house prices in more detail. It's easy to become nervous, so let's look at the long-term trends. After all, we're in property for the long term – it's a marathon, not a sprint.

---

3 https://www.ons.gov.uk/economy/inflationandpriceindices /bulletins/housepriceindex/feb2017
4 http://www.telegraph.co.uk/property/house-prices/the-state-of-t he-uk-housing-market-in-five-charts/

Sold house price data has been recorded by the Land Registry since 1 January 1995. From then until the most recent data release (March 2016), the average property selling prices have increased from £108,000 for all house types (detached, semi-detached, terraced and flats) to £580,330 – a whopping 437% return over the period.

What about during the downturn from May 2008 to March 2009? What's interesting is the difference between the average and the median prices. They tell a slightly different story. (For more information about mean and average house prices versus median house prices, visit the Realestate.com website.[5])

For simplicity, we'll focus on the average house prices, as I believe they more accurately reflect what happens in the market. The value of top end of the market (detached homes) fell by 20% in the period from May 2008 to March 2009. Terraced houses dropped by 11%, while semis and flats lost 7% of their value. The overall decline was 7%. Volumes also dropped off, with the number of transactions falling by over 40% during the same period.

It's difficult to paint an accurate picture borough by borough, because sales were so thin. It's fair to say that prices in Belgravia, one of the most expensive boroughs in central London,

---

5  http://www.realestate.com.au/advice/median-house-price-what -does-it-mean/.

fell by over 15% in the period when the UK experienced its biggest price drop.

The Home.co.uk website has a great tool for looking at changes in house prices over any period between January 1995 and the date of the most recent Land Registry data[6].

What about these naysayers declaring the doom and gloom of London house prices with drops of up to 40%? I'm sceptical. Brexit was another blow to premium house prices in the capital – along with the stamp duty increases of 1 April 2016 – but its real impact has been an 18% drop in sterling against the US dollar. Our real estate is on sale.

Savills reported in their full-year financial report that the result of this house-price sale has led to more Asian and European investors. Luckily for Savills, the knock-on effect was a healthy full-year result. Domestic-focused agents haven't been so lucky.

Individual properties might drop by 30% due to the circumstances of the seller, and the top end of the market might suffer at the expense of the lower end. But remember, trend is your friend. The long-term house price trend is upward and you won't benefit if you're not on the ladder.

---

6 http://www.home.co.uk/guides/house_prices_report.htm
?location=london&all=1

In most cases, it's not plummeting prices that wipe out developers. Bankruptcies occur when developers overleverage and lenders recall loans. I've written more about this in Chapter Four (see the section on finance). I strongly believe that in the 2008 downturn many lenders behaved irresponsibly, worsening the financial crisis. Banks could have avoided much of the heartache by taking a more pragmatic, long-term approach, allowing the developer to continue with the development and selling out once prices recovered. Until the lenders have learned their lesson, the onus is on the developer to be prudent in their debt levels.

# WHAT THIS BOOK IS NOT

This is not a book about how to get rich quick. I'm not selling the millionaire dream or course. I'm not an expert – in fact, I have no formal education in property.

While I will share my knowledge with you, this book is the story of how I scaled up my property business from the initial investment of £1 million to investing several million in over £120 million of development.

I've learned everything I know in property by teaming up with people who are more experienced than me and learning from their experiences. Whether you're a complete beginner or a seasoned professional, I hope there are ideas in this book that you'll be able to use in your own property career.

I have not written a step-by-step guide, as things in property are changing all the time in line with legislation and trends. My goal is that you can learn from my experiences and apply some of this to your own property journey.

# The Beginning

## My Background

I want to share my background with you so you can see just how ordinary I am. Although I started with over £1 million of savings earned from years of banking, I wasn't born with a silver spoon and my parents weren't actively involved in property. I didn't marry a rich man. In fact, my story is quite the opposite.

Growing up in Australia, I couldn't have told you if my family were working class or middle class. Both my parents were nurses and with four children, money was tight. My parents always built their own homes, or at least extended them. My father worked alongside the 'tradies' when his nursing schedule allowed. We spent Saturday afternoons driving around new housing estates in the suburbs of Sydney, admiring the homogenous houses springing up on what was once farmland. Apart from that, I had no exposure to property.

Later we moved away from the city to start a new life. My parents invested everything in a 50-acre hobby farm in the hinterland of Coffs Harbour, New South Wales. We had fifty head of beef cattle, a few horses, various other animals and a couple of dirt bikes. We lived in a caravan park, and then a large industrial shed on our property, while my parents slowly built their dream home.

We lived in the shed until a mud slide triggered by a flash flood washed away our living areas and most of our belongings. Mum put her foot down and demanded that we moved into the house in its current half-built state. I clearly remember having makeshift brick islands throughout the kitchen and dining area. As kids, we didn't mind the temporary flooring and plastic-sheeted windows. It was an adventure. In hindsight, it must have been horrendous for my parents.

The burden of working in a demanding job, a hectic family life and interest rates of 17% took their toll on my parents' finances and their marriage. It wasn't long before the dream became the nightmare and my parents divorced.

With everything invested in this dream property, money was even tighter. My three brothers and I moved with my mother into a rental property in a bad neighbourhood close to the centre of Coffs Harbour. I was highly impressed when our young landlord brought us a bottle of wine for Christmas. I decided that that was the kind of landlord I would be.

As a full-time sole parent to children aged from 3 to 13, my mother couldn't work until my youngest brother started school. We survived on benefits and a bit of cash that my mum earned for cleaning houses. Because my mother didn't drink or smoke and we didn't eat meat, she managed to put three of us through private school for a couple of years each. I remember that often, by the end of each fortnight we'd be eating banana sandwiches and one-dollar hot chips from the local takeaway while we waited for her benefits to clear. When I was a bit older my mother was able to return to working nights as a nurse while I babysat my brothers.

I remember my mother spending her evenings bent over calculations in notebooks, budgeting all the money each fortnight down to the last cent. There was no room for error.

At age 14 I got my first job at McDonald's, as many Australian teenagers do. It's a brilliant training ground and in some ways I'm disappointed that my children won't experience the same thing. I worked twenty to thirty hours a week at two different restaurants to earn enough money to buy extras. I was really careful with my money, saving everything for clothes and travel. Priorities!

Earning money was always a priority – unfortunately, to the detriment of my education. I didn't do that badly though, and I was awarded a scholarship to boarding school in Melbourne for Year 11. I struggled through the last year of school begrudging the fact that I couldn't leave and work full-time.

After my final year of school, I managed to get into a pre-med university course on the Gold Coast, Queensland. With only fourteen hours a week of contact time, I got a part-time job at a haberdashery factory packing orders. Still finding that I had spare time, I also stacked shelves at a department store. It was too much though, and I was physically exhausted and struggling to keep up with university. I got fired from the factory for sleeping through my alarm. Living away from home wasn't cheap, so after a couple of semesters I switched to distance learning so I could focus on working.

I took a full-time job as a receptionist and research assistant at a stockbroking firm in Brisbane. This experience opened my eyes. I'd never met anyone rich before. Now I was working alongside people I believed to be really wealthy. They wore nice suits, drove nice cars and lived in the good suburbs. I knew then that I wanted to make money – serious money. I didn't want to struggle and count every cent like my parents had to.

My boss, Mark Arnold, told me that after you make the first $300,000 in cash the rest comes more easily. Making as much as that seemed like an impossible dream at that time: I was earning $16,500 a year. In the last week before payday I'd be eating vegemite on toast for breakfast, lunch and dinner. But it gave me the hunger to succeed. It's a yearning that's hard to put into words.

While working and studying for university, I studied for the Chartered Financial Planner qualification, managing to become the youngest qualified independent financial adviser in Australia. I had started to build a solid base for my future. My boyfriend at the time, Matt, had recently returned from twelve months' travelling through Europe and Asia. It sounded so exotic. I was torn. I wanted to succeed and make money, but the draw of Europe was too strong.

As part of my plan for global success, I packed up all my belongings in my Suzuki Sierra (Google it – a great little car) and moved to Sydney. I soon managed to land a new job with a 100% pay rise at another stockbroking firm. It wasn't long before I met Michael, a young equities analyst who worked even harder than me and had the most incredible, steely discipline. I often joke that I had a list of what I wanted in a man – tall, dark, muscular, educated, European – and he met every checkbox except one: he was blonde. As a German with family still there, Michael was keen to return to Europe. I was in love.

After just a couple of months together, Michael was transferred to London. Even though I'd just turned 22 and hadn't finished my degree I jumped at the chance of a European adventure. I arrived in London in December 2000 wearing a thin cotton coat, on a working holiday visa without more than £100 to my name. What I did have was a burning desire to succeed in banking.

Unfortunately, it was much harder than I expected. The year 2001 was when the tech bubble burst. My financial-planning qualifications were worthless in the UK and I didn't have much work experience. Despite this, by March I was sponsored by CAIB, an Austrian bank. But that summer, CAIB was taken over by the larger Bank Austria and I was made redundant. Being made redundant the way banks do it – having security escort you out of the building with a box of your belongings – is traumatic and soul-destroying. But it was even worse: I'd lost my work visa. After less than a year I was facing being deported and leaving the man I loved. It didn't cross my mind that Michael would happily support me. I had to be independent.

I spent my unemployed days working out at the gym. I was in great shape, but I was miserable. Michael was getting worried about me too and suggested that I should return home. I couldn't. That would have been defeat.

The manager at my gym felt sorry for me and gave me a cash-in-hand job picking up dirty towels off the gym floor and tidying the changing rooms. It's amazing how invisible I became to the members of this inner-city London gym. It was my first experience of the class system in the UK and it was ugly. It was a degrading experience, but it kept me occupied and I made money while my lawyer worked out what to do with my visa.

Eventually my luck changed and I managed to qualify for the Highly Skilled Migrant visa. With my residency status sorted out, I could look for work once again. That's when I landed my dream job as an equity research associate at Capital Asset Management, the largest fund manager in the world at the time. I really did enjoy my time there. I made some great friends and my eyes were opened all over again about true wealth. I even got to travel to Los Angeles for business.

After a couple of years, it was clear that professionally my job wasn't all I'd hoped for. The work was stimulating, but in the corporate world I had no control over my career. It was firmly in the hands of my managers, who had little interest in progressing me as quickly as I needed to. With some uncertainty, I left Capital to set up my own business, which gave me a taste of entrepreneurship.

# The Start of My Property Journey

In 2004 Michael and I purchased a flat in Clerkenwell. It was on the main road, which always irked me, being a light sleeper. But it had a good café on the ground floor and it was within walking distance of the City and West End. When we moved to New York we became accidental landlords, renting out the property and managing the tenants. I came to dread the emails from the tenants complaining that the shower wasn't hanging straight or there were no instructions for the oven (hadn't they heard of Google?). I knew that being a landlord of single properties wasn't for me.

Upon our return, our flat wasn't suitable for our growing family. It was a duplex flat with steep stairs and a balcony that was completely unsuitable for two children under two years of age. We gave the tenants notice and called in some builders to renovate the flat, which was looking a little tired after being tenanted for a couple of years. It was such an easy process. I took on a couple of Polish painters who could do everything, told them what colour to paint the walls (not magnolia) and visited once a week until the to-do list was complete. We then listed it on the market.

To our astonishment, in the six years we owned the flat its value had almost doubled, and we sold it for over £800,000. Little did I know at the time, but this was my first taste of property development and gave me the funds I needed for my first investment property.

After returning from the US we were actively looking for a family home. Unlike our friends, we refused to commute across London from the west to work in the City. I wanted to live as close to Michael's work as possible to maximise his precious family time. The search for inexpensive space led us to Hackney, somewhere we'd not considered before. Even walking through London Fields during the day was a scary proposition.

Much to the amusement of our friends, I liked the vibe in Hackney back in 2010. It felt so young and fresh, so raw with opportunity. Best of all, it was a fifteen-minute commute for Michael and I could run in Victoria Park. We rented an old Victorian semi on the picturesque Albion Square and started to look to buy.

In early 2010 I was walking my two toddlers to nursery when

I saw a hand-painted 'for sale' sign above the garden wall of a crumbling house. I couldn't believe I hadn't clocked the house before under the overgrown Virginia creeper. The next morning, I noticed that the hand-painted sign had been replaced by a Foxtons sign.

By 8.30am I had called and arranged a viewing for noon the same day, and I even managed to get Michael home from work.

I like to think I don't get emotional about property, but this house took my breath away. To call it a fixer-upper is an understatement. As I walked through the door I actually choked up (with emotion, not the bad smell). An arched entrance gave way to a large hall with a grand staircase curving around to the next floor. The rooms off the hall were huge, with high ceilings and solid timber floors.

Upstairs the surprises continued, with eight large bedrooms. I pretended not to notice as the agent, James, kicked a used condom under a bed.

The potential was huge. What sealed it for me was going down to the basement and seeing the arched coal cellar under the stairs. I pictured escaping from the chaos of the kids to sip a brandy and puff a cigar – neither of which I partake of, but I liked the image.

James left me to plead my case with Michael. By 4pm Michael had worked on his appraisal, counted our money and made an offer. The vendor extracted an extra £50,000 from us to take it off the market, and by 8pm we were under offer. With the benefit of experience, it's surprising that the conveyancing went without a hitch. By summer we were the owners of a 4,000 square foot former vicarage with crumbling bricks, peeling lead paint and rotten windows.

I didn't know it at the time, but this was the next important step in my property journey. It would take my career to a level I had never dreamed possible.

## My First Property

Thankfully, I don't really remember the day-to-day problems of each development, including my first as a professional property developer – Lenthall Road. When I look back it's only the positives that have stayed fresh in my mind. My first property certainly didn't go to plan. We had an issue with one neighbour (more on that later), our budget overran by about £90,000 and our timescale overran by three months.

Damian, my builder, was as green as I was. We tried to schedule things and it worked most of the time. By the end, though,

I was growing frustrated with the slipping schedule and haemorrhaging cash. I just wanted to get on with the next project. But I had to sell this one first.

It was all hands on deck. During these earlier years I was quite hands-on, much to the amusement of my guys. I tried painting once, but they politely but firmly took the brush out of my hand and tried to fix the damage I'd done. I was quite good at painting the stain onto the floors though, so I was left with that task. And the landscaping: I planted hundreds of shrubs and trees in the borders of the 108-foot garden, laid the turf, laid the paving and spread the gravel. One balmy summer evening I even convinced my close friend Helen to help me spread gravel on the front garden in exchange for beers, before the council fined me for having a pallet in the parking bay. I'm eternally grateful to the friends who helped me out like this and to the builders, who worked into the early hours seven days a week to meet the deadline.

I was still staging the property on the morning of the open day – much to the disgust of the agent, who had a dozen viewers queuing at the front of the property. It managed to sell in ten days to a French family who wanted to escape an increase in taxes. They even invited me to their housewarming party.

Other properties followed Lenthall Road. At the time, the goal was to complete one or two houses a year and safely build up my pot. But then I met Avi. Our meeting in October 2013 was the biggest turning point in my property career. I learned about development finance and joint ventures: the two tools that let me scale up my business so quickly.

In 2016 I was working on my cash flow model when it occurred to me that I was working on over £100 million of property in gross development value. I didn't own all the properties, but I was operating them all with Avi and I had some skin in every deal. It was one of the few times in my life that I allowed myself to feel proud of this huge milestone I'd achieved in just over three years.

# Three Key Factors

## Joint Ventures

Joint ventures enabled me to scale up my property portfolio so rapidly. That's it. No fancy strategy I could sell you a course to learn. Just working with other people. But not just anyone: I worked with someone who was more experienced than I was. By working with Avi in a joint venture, I was able to learn on the project and piggyback off his experience, expertise and contacts.

My first joint venture nearly didn't happen. Rob (not his real name), an old friend based abroad, had heard about the success we'd had on the first couple of projects and decided he wanted to invest. He had £1 million sitting in a UK bank account with a paltry interest rate and owned a couple of investment properties in London.

I sent him an investment pack for a property I'd found on Englefield Road in Islington. It was an HMO that had been owned by the same family for decades. It was in a terrible state and I'd hardly wanted to touch the doors to open them when I viewed it – the perfect property. There was one room we couldn't get into on the first viewing. During the second visit I insisted that we inspect it, so the vendor reluctantly opened the door. In the middle of the studio flat was a bed made up with black satin sheets. A video camera sat on a tripod and professional lighting focused on the bed. I quickly backed out of the door, trying not to touch anything.

My initial calculations showed that I could buy the property for the asking price of £1.4 million, spend another £250,000 on renovations and sell it for around £2 million. This would be a nice profit for a year's work. Rob agreed and we went ahead with the purchase.

The transaction was going smoothly until the day of the exchange. I received a call from Rob, saying 'I'm sorry, Nicole, but I'm not comfortable with this transaction. I can't do it'. I was floored. I knew it was a great property in a good area. In late 2013, prices were on fire in the Islington and Hackney areas. I didn't want to miss out, but I didn't have the full £1.4 million I needed to buy the property myself.

Disappointed, I rang my architect, Amrita Mahindroo of Droo Projects. Amrita had put in a lot of work on the plans for Englefield Road and she knew it was a great project. She told me to hold tight, as she might have someone who was interested. Minutes later I got a call from Avi Dodi. He asked more about the property, the area and my plans for the construction. In hindsight, I cringe at how green I must have sounded. But Avi could tell it was a great deal and he wasn't put off by my inexperience. We agreed to meet at the property the next afternoon.

For the first and only time in our years of working together, Avi was on time. I was about thirty minutes late, having lost track of time as I lunched with the Sister Snog sisters. We shook hands while the agent and vendor eyed us suspiciously, not knowing what to make of the situation. Together we walked into the basement flat. Avi looked around with his experienced eye and said, 'Let's do it'.

At the time, I was shocked that Avi agreed so quickly. A couple of years later, one of his site managers told me that they had arrived early and found a loose board across a window so they did their own unauthorised inspection before I got there. At the time, I was highly impressed. In our fourth year of working together, I know that Avi is highly decisive: an admirable quality in someone you're in partnership with.

Michael was sceptical when I told him I was going to invest hundreds of thousands of pounds in a property with a person I'd just met. But we went out to dinner with Avi and his wife, at Tsunami, an excellent Japanese restaurant on Charlotte Street. It turned out that Avi owned a founding stake in the business. We had a great evening; Michael asked Avi about his development experience while we all got to know each other. I felt confident that I could work well with Avi and, more importantly, that I could learn so much from him. At the end of the evening I signed the exchange documents and the shareholders' agreement.

This wasn't my only due diligence on Avi, though. I ordered Companies House reports on his companies and spoke to some of his employees. I was impressed that many had worked with him for decades. He was a firm but direct boss who didn't suffer fools, but he was generous and he rewarded loyalty and efficiency.

It took us a while to build trust, get into a rhythm with our communication and establish roles. It wasn't all smooth sailing and there were times when we were frustrated with each other, especially because of my lack of knowledge. But Avi respected the fact that I'd brought him a property that he otherwise wouldn't have had the opportunity to develop. He appreciated that I was prepared to get in and help wherever possible.

Those first few months of working with Avi were intense. This was just one of dozens of projects he had on the go, but I had only two. There were quite a few synergies between the two, so I could apply everything I was learning on Englefield Road to my second property on Parkholme Road.

One of the first things Avi taught me was that I wasn't thinking big enough about Englefield Road. He believed that if we increased our development budget to £600,000, we could achieve £1,000 a square foot in sales value. That's over £3 million. I wasn't convinced, but was willing to go along with it.

The second lesson was development finance. I hadn't realised that bank finance was available to smaller developers. Avi set up the finance with the Royal Bank of Scotland (RBS). This meant we only had to find about £600,000 of the full purchase and development costs, which left me money for my next purchase.

Part way through the Englefield Road project, a friend and fellow developer showed me a roof space with planning permission for three luxury flats on City Road. It was listed for sale at offers over £2 million. She was keen to buy the property as a joint venture with me and Avi, as he had experience in developing roof spaces. He also had access to cheap bank finance, rather than the costly bridging lending that she had previously worked with.

The views were spectacular across south London toward the London Eye, The Shard (which wasn't yet completed), and to the neighbouring large developments on the north side of City Road. While still on the roof space with the developer, I texted details to Avi. I had only just hit send when he called to ask if the agent could wait half an hour for him to view. (I now call this my Avi indicator. If I send him a property and he responds straight away, it's a good one. If he doesn't respond at all, it's not and I leave it.)

Avi could tell that the property had the potential to go up another level, doubling the square footage and the profits. Avi left my friend to do the negotiating, but with her best and final offer of £2.1 million, we were going to miss out. When Avi decides he wants a property, he doesn't like losing. He knew the people at Estate Office and he knew the freeholders of the building. After a twelve-hour exchange race (two solicitors against the clock to see who can finalise the conveyancing first and exchange), we managed to win with a purchase price of £2.2 million. This was too high for the other developer to make it work and she left the property to me and Avi.

In some ways, this was a good move by the developer. I had nearly £1 million of cash tied up in the deal while we fought for the right to add an additional level. But it's also a shame, because this property has been a game-changer for me: the GDP is over £12 million with costs of £4 million.

At the time of writing, we're in the construction planning stage. This is complicated and we need to do months of planning before we start the work. Londoners are going to hate us when we block City Road with a crane to lift the pre-fabricated steel structure onto the roof!

I'm sure you're curious about how Avi and I fared on our first joint venture, Englefield Road. After leaving the property on the market for a few months, we sold it for £3.2 million, just £500,000 under the asking price, to a young musician who fell in love with the property. We were shortlisted for the International Design and Architecture Award for our work on the property, which is a testament to Amrita's skill as an architect and interior designer.

I was lucky to meet a great joint venture partner like Avi. It's not always that easy. In fact, I'm approached regularly by people who see our success and want to be part of it. I would work with many of these people if the opportunity arose, but it's important to be careful when you're choosing who to work with.

At the end of 2016 I was approached by a man whose name I won't mention. He claimed to have secured a couple of really great projects that I'd been eyeing in Hackney and Tower Hamlets. But things didn't seem quite right. They just weren't adding up. And he spent far too much time on the phone name-dropping and talking about his girlfriend.

After tolerating this for a couple of months, I pulled him up on some inaccuracies in his story. He let loose with a barrage of abuse. This shook me, but true colours come out. You have to like who you work with. I didn't leave the corporate world, where I had no control over my colleagues, to work with people I don't like. And it's not just about personality.

Recently I was in discussion with a potential investor and solicitor. We got along well and he was ready to invest a considerable sum, but he was making changes to our contracts that were in his favour but not in the favour of our other investor. He also wanted us to underwrite the downside risk and then take all the upside himself. Investment doesn't work like that. If you want the high returns you have to take the downside risks. I politely told him that I didn't believe it would work out at this time but the door was always open if he wished to invest at a later time. And I hope he will.

Once you start experiencing some successes, beware of those who want to align themselves with your brand. It's your brand

and your reputation. Don't tolerate those who you don't instantly warm to. Trust your first instinct.

# How to Find Joint Venture Partners

How can you find good joint venture partners? For the first few projects before teaming up with Avi, my partners and investors were friends. They'd ask what I was doing or see my posts on Facebook and decide they wanted to be part of it.

From late 2015 I started speaking on what's known as the property circuit. I attended an informal coffee morning hosted by Brendan Quinn from Central London Property Meet. There I met a lovely fellow Aussie, Dean Morrison. Dean has a portfolio of high-end HMOs and talked me through a new area that I knew little about. It was my first property networking meet-up and Dean put me at ease. I shared with him what I was working on. Impressed, Dean later told Brendan that I'd be a good speaker for one of his events. Brendan told Elsie Igbinadolor, who runs the Women in Property and Business networking meeting, and Elsie asked me to speak at her October 2015 event. This was a key turning point in my career.

Up until that point, I'd never even been able to ask a question in public without sweating and stammering. I couldn't believe I'd said yes to Elsie. I'd also never even attended one of these large networking meetings before, so I didn't know what to expect. I decided that the best strategy was to tell my story.

People reading from a PowerPoint presentation is one of my pet peeves – I can read it myself! I was determined to use PowerPoint only to show pictures of my development and to be transparent about the financials. These would be my prompts and I wouldn't need notes. I figured that if I just told my story, I couldn't go wrong.

My strategy worked and I surprised myself by how calmly I presented to Elsie's friendly group of about sixty women gathered at the Holiday Inn in Mayfair. I spoke for well over an hour and the questions kept coming. From that point I was hooked on the buzz I got from speaking.

Word got around that there was 'fresh blood' on the circuit and I was booked every month for all of 2016 – sometimes more than once a month. I thoroughly enjoyed it and loved meeting all the interesting people at these events. Of course, I was inundated with requests to invest with me.

There's an important piece of legislation about taking invest-ment, or even discussing investing, with retail investors or the public. This means that you can't even speak to a potential investor about investing until you've established that they're a sophisticated or high net worth investor. For this reason, I turned away most of the offers.

It's essential that you review the Financial Conduct Authority's (FCA) publication on the legislation around who you can and cannot discuss potential investments with. (For the full document[7])

In summary:

- As a developer you are not to present potential investments to retail investors, only to professional investors or sophisticated, high net worth (HNW) investors.

- A professional investor is a person who typically is in the business of investing.

- A sophisticated investor has extensive knowledge of complex investments.

- A HNW investor has an income of over £100,000 or investable assets of over £250,000.

- A retail investor is one who does not fall into one of the categories above.

---

7 https://www.fca.org.uk/publication/policy/ps13-03.pdf.

If you can't speak to potential investors unless you've ascertained their status, how do you find them? Turn the question around: what problems do most savers have? The bank offers them a dismal return, they've maxed out their ISAs and premium bonds, and they have a couple of properties, which are managed for them. They work full-time but want access to the returns of 10% or more that are available in property development. You can solve that problem for them. You just need to be able to show that you have been successful in the past and that you have the systems in place to meet their needs. Once you can show this, people will come to you with more funds than you can allocate. This is the problem that I currently have – it's not a bad one, is it?

How do you demonstrate your ability to solve their problem? Get your name out there. Speak at events, get on social media (I'll discuss that later in this chapter) and go to events like Property Fortress. Chat with people online at Property Tribes, Twitter and Facebook, create a lovely website, and run tours of your properties. This will solidify your position as a reputable property developer who people will want to work with. But only if you really are that person.

Don't pretend to be what you're not. People will see straight through it. Your reputation is on the line. Guard it fiercely and operate with the highest level of integrity and transparency. If you do this, your investors will be the same.

# Crowdfunding

When I spoke at property events, people continually asked me how they could take part in my projects. Because of the FCA PS13/3 requirements discussed previously, I couldn't accept anything under £250,000. But I felt strongly that people with smaller amounts should have the same opportunity as larger investors.

It was my broker who came up with a solution: crowdfunding, the ultimate joint venture. This was something I'd considered before. I thought a good business model would be for a crowdfunding platform to outsource its regulatory and back-end systems to property developers so developers could offer branded crowdfunding on their own websites. It's a similar model to hedge funds. Many crowdfunding platforms aren't directly regulated by the Financial Conduct Authority (FCA) but outsource that function to a platform that is regulated. The fund pays a fee for the service. No one does this yet for property. If they ever do, you heard it here first.

My broker pointed out that crowdfunding via an FCA-regulated platform would protect my investors and allow me to work with people who want to invest as little as £500. It seemed like the perfect solution to my problem, not to mention a great PR opportunity for my brand.

My broker arranged a meeting with Atuksha and Davin Poonwassie, founders of Simple Equity, a crowdfunding platform for property developers and investors. I instantly warmed to them. I could tell that they genuinely care about their investors and developers and operate with the level of integrity that is important to me.

Not long into our meeting I decided to crowdfund Dalston Lane, a site we'd exchanged contracts on in Hackney and the home of St. Matthias Youth Club. It's a great project, given the location and the potential profit. Importantly, I'd already lined up £1.2 million of the £1.4 million equity I needed to raise. It would be a safe project to go live with, starting the relationship in a positive way.

Listing Dalston Lane with Simple Equity was a fairly straightforward process. I submitted the legal documents on the ownership and purchase of the property, our shareholder agreement template and our investment proposal. Simple Equity carried out the client checks and anti-money-laundering processes, collected funds and, once everything was complete, paid the money into our bank accounts.

Although I had already lined up £1.2 million in investment from some larger investors, you never know if they're going to invest until the time comes. It was an ambitious target, but I raised £1.4 million in just nine days. I could have raised over £2 million if we needed it, as the demand was so strong.

On this project, Avi and I still had to put in equity. We don't want to raise 100% of the equity requirement; we like our projects and we want to invest too. It gives our investors comfort that we believe enough in our developments to want to invest in them. For Dalston Lane, Avi and I put in £300,000 in total. This isn't always possible though, as we don't have endless pots of cash. Crowdfunding was a game-changer for the way we raised equity; we could get almost instant commitments from investors.

Here are some tips for successful crowdfunding:

- Have a designer prepare an investor pack that looks professional.

- Try to line up as much of the equity as possible before the raise so you can hit the ground running. In crowdfunding there are psychological barriers – people want to see that 50% of the target has been raised before they invest. Once it hits 70%, people are more likely to invest. Try to get it to 50% before you list your project.

- Consider offering tours of the property. With our second crowdfunding (for Harrington Gardens), this made a huge difference. People like to be able to see the property.

- Opening bank accounts and raising debt can be a nightmare if you have twenty-eight different investors, so incorporate the company with just one or two directors and shareholders first. Open your bank account and raise the debt with just these one or two people. Once that's done, add the new shareholders to the company with Companies House. It will save you so much time and effort.

- Have a solicitor draft up a tight shareholder agreement specifically for crowdfunding. This not only looks professional but can also protect you if things go wrong. Make sure you have clauses in place so that you as the developer cannot be voted out as a director. This is particularly important if you are a minority shareholder after the crowdfunding. While it would be stupid of the crowd to vote you out, it could happen. Don't change the shareholder agreement for a single investor. I had a solicitor who wanted to invest but insisted on a number of changes. Don't do it. It has to be the same for all investors.

- Continually communicate with your investors. Set their expectations from the outset about what communications they'll receive: how often, what and how. Do they expect monthly accounts? If you've set their expectations, you have to deliver or they'll think you're hiding something. Do they hate email? A more efficient way could be to set up a system like Basecamp, where investors can log in and see the management system in process. It doesn't matter how you do it, as long as you set up a process, keep your promises and communicate when investors expect. The moment you miss a deadline, doubts will begin to surface and investors will start to question your every move.

- Invite investors on tours of their property as often as is practical. This lets them see the progress, understand the time it takes and appreciate the 'before and after' so much more. Most people don't understand how much work goes into a development – so show them! This will make them appreciate you more; they might decide that development isn't for them after all and they should let you do the hard work. I've certainly been told this before.

- At the end of the project, wind up the accounts as quickly as possible. Pay back your investors and celebrate. It will have been a tumultuous few months. Celebrate the successes, no matter how small.

What if you're not yet a developer? Why should you consider crowdfunding a project? Think of it as a joint venture. If you're working with the right developer, they'll let you get involved to some extent. They should at least give you full insight into the process so you can learn as you go. This gives you the opportunity to piggyback off the developer's experience in the same way I did with Avi years ago. This is so much more than passive investing. It's a way of funding your own education while (hopefully) making a decent return. Why sink

£30,000 into a course that talks hypothetically about investing in property when you could invest it in a property through a crowdfunding platform and learn from the developers while making a return? It seems like a no-brainer to me.

What if you don't yet own your own home? Is crowdfunding still an option? Absolutely. I think about it like trading futures on the futures exchange. Remember all those people wearing coloured jackets and making secret hand gestures? They were trading futures. For example, if you're running an airline and you think that fuel prices are going to go up over the next twelve months, why not buy your fuel now at the current price? You don't have to find anywhere to store it or take delivery of it for another twelve months; you just lock in the price. You would buy a futures contract and lock in the delivery of tonnes of fuel at today's prices. You pay a transaction fee to the broker for the privilege, but that's nothing compared to the savings you'll make on the fuel.

There are people who take this a step further. They're sitting at their desks at home or in a bank. They're never expecting to take delivery of fuel, palladium or pork bellies, but they think that prices are going to rise. So they buy a futures contract to lock in the price. They can then sell this contract for a profit – before 100 tonnes of pork bellies are delivered to their office.

The same concept applies to property. Say you can't afford

the 28% deposit that the average first-time buyer needs to put down to buy a house, but you believe that prices are going up. How do you take advantage of the rising prices? You buy a small contract on a property through crowdfunding. You then get to lock in your investment at today's prices and take advantage of the increase. Getting exposure to the property market for as little as £500 and learning on the way? I'd want to do it.

# Building a Brand

Attracting investment requires a strong brand presence. Even if you're raising debt for your first project, the lender will require a development CV and will certainly look at your website and your LinkedIn and Facebook profiles. They want to get a glimpse of you and, like it or not, you'll be judged on what's out there.

Branding agencies will take you through a full programme to develop your brand. These might be worthwhile if you're clueless, but most people can come up with a basic overview of who they are, what they stand for and how they want to be seen in the market.

Spend some time considering these points. Write down your

values and vision. This will be the basis of your brand. It will dictate your business name, logo design and even the colours the designer will use.

Finding the right name for your business isn't easy. I struggled, and sometimes still struggle, with this. Sometimes I think East Eight is too localised and London Central Developments too long. But East Eight is a heritage brand – it tells the story of where I've come from. If you've got a memorable surname, use that as your brand. Ask people. Be prepared to get as many different views as the number of people you question.

Once you have a business name, hire a designer to develop a logo. It's important to get this right, as it will be on everything you touch – business cards, letterhead, website and social media platforms. The moment people see your logo they'll think of you, so spend some cash.

With your logo and business cards sorted, you're ready for a website. Websites only have a shelf life of twelve to eighteen months before they need refreshing, so I don't spend more than £2,000 at a time on mine. It's just a place where people can go to see who you are and what you do and look at your portfolio. In the age of social media, websites aren't used as much as they once were.

Now you're ready to start promoting your brand. You need

to get out there and have people know who you are and what you're doing.

# Speaking

Speaking on the property networking circuit was my magic bullet for building brand awareness. The organisers would promote me across social media before the event, reaching thousands of people. At the event I'd have twenty minutes to an hour to share my story with dozens, or even hundreds, of people. Even paid advertising doesn't get you that sort of exposure.

For that reason, be careful where you speak and who is aligning themselves with your brand. Protect your name at all costs. Be sure that you're only speaking at events where your values match those of the organiser. It's hard to recover once you've been tarred with the same brush as someone else.

Public speaking is stressful for many people. I would find myself sweating and hyperventilating just to ask a question in a crowded room. Being prepared and doing some visualisation exercises before the event were the best ways for me to cope. I also had some great coaching by a speaking coach. He showed me that people are most interested in my story.

Better still, how can you mess up a talk if it's just your story? You know it. You've lived it.

The worst thing you can do is get up on stage stammering and have people feel sorry for you. Pretend you're chatting with a small group at a restaurant about what you're doing. Throw away the notes and just tell your story. Don't worry if you miss bits out or need to backtrack. Just talk. Like everything, you'll get better with practice.

## Social Media

On the days we work at home together, Michael gets frustrated with me because I'm on my phone all the time. I tell him it's work. Yep, playing around with Facebook and Snapchat is time well spent. Believe it or not, these are the places where I connect with most of my investors and joint venture partners.

I don't have that many followers, but it's not about quantity. Social media is all about quality: depth of engagement, not breadth.

There's plenty about engagement in this section, because that's the secret of all social media interaction. It's not about being a PR machine broadcasting how great you and your brand are and shouting about all your wins. It's about engaging with people and forming genuine relationships.

Business today isn't just about promoting your product or service and hoping people will do business with you. People want to buy into *you*. They want to get to know you and buy into who you are. This means people want to see the real you. Not just the polished Instagram version, but the real Facebook Live and Snapchat person.

Marketing is about touchpoints and getting people to trust you as your brand. By being active across social media platforms, you're giving people the opportunity to touch your brand and build a relationship with you. This builds trust in your brand, and in you. Once a potential joint venture partner has invested in getting to know you – your likes, your dislikes and even a bit about your family – it's harder for them to do business with someone they haven't invested this much time in.

There's a myriad of social media experts out there, but the most important thing, which no expert can teach you, is to be authentic and use your own voice. Don't be like anyone else out there. Be your own brilliant self. That's who your potential partners are buying into.

Remember, it doesn't have to be perfect. It doesn't even

need to look professional. Just get it out there. Mix in some professional content and you'll really start to engage with your audience.

## Facebook

Facebook is about building communities, showing the polished and unpolished design and having conversations. Most social media experts will say that this is where the focus should be. With over 1.7 billion users, it's the most used platform in the world so it's one you need to be on.

**FACEBOOK LIVE**: Facebook Live is where you need to be in this video-centric world. Don't worry about how you come across – this is how you look and sound in everyday life. Scary, right? As with anything, you just have to do it. Once you've done it a couple of times, it gets easier and you'll be less self-conscious. And don't worry about how few people join you for the live sessions. Many more will watch afterwards.

**PERSONAL PROFILE OR PAGE**: When I first set up my Facebook account I was living in New York and used it as a way to connect with family and friends abroad. It was just pictures of the kids and their achievements. When I started speaking at events and meeting new people I started receiving friend requests from business associates. At first I would ignore them and then add them on LinkedIn if I could find them. Then I realised that people expected me to connect with them. I was limiting my number of contacts and my potential to connect with the right people.

I really struggled with how much of my family to put on my profile. I also struggled with how much of my business life I bombarded my family and friends with. For me, nothing is more annoying than people constantly banging their business drum on their personal Facebook page.

After much thought I set up a fan page (yes, it makes me cringe just writing it) for people who are not close friends or family. This means I can share my kids' achievements with my family (lucky them) without worrying that I'm overexposing my children. I can also share business wins on Facebook without annoying those who don't want to see them. The other benefit is that while personal pages have a 5,000 friend limit, a fan page has no limit. It's scalable in so many ways. Use it like a business page (see below) but with a more personal slant.

I've connected with so many people on Facebook, and other social platforms, who I haven't met in person. At a recent property awards dinner, it felt like I was in a living Facebook. All around me were people I knew only as a smiling face on their Facebook profile, walking around and saying hello. It was a new experience that was indicative of the social media age we live in.

BUSINESS PAGE: For the same reason as you set up your fan page, you should also have a business page so you're not bombarding your friends and family with your business life. They can opt in by liking your business page. I have East Eight and London Central Developments pages for this purpose. I rarely share business posts on my personal page or vice versa. It creates a separation.

What should you put on your business page? Everything related to property. It should be visual. It can relate to your business and to property in general. It can be as micro as talking about the neighbourhood you're developing in, including local delis and shops. It can be as macro as global house prices or holiday destinations. Talk about architecture, interior design, construction methods – anything property-related. Show the progress of your developments, including key team members, and then the finished products. Use a mix of polished pictures, unpolished pictures, edited videos, and videos taken on your phone over the top of building noise. Make it as broad as possible to engage as many people as you can.

If you have a really good post that seems to be getting a lot of attention, boost it using Facebook advertising. Spend a little money to get it out there to other potential investors and joint venture partners. Facebook provides detailed insight into your post views and engagements, so use it to see what's working and what's not working so well. Continue to play around and refine your strategy. Gradually your numbers will grow.

GROUPS: No matter what you're into, there's a Facebook group for it. You can find a group of people who are into the same obscure hobby as you and chat to them every day. With property, there are hundreds of groups you can join to engage with like-minded people. Ask questions, answer questions, discuss deals and moan about builders, valuations and banks. Most groups have strict guidelines on self-promotion, but by being active in the groups you'll build kudos and people will want to engage with you.

What about setting up your own group? That sounds scary to me. Groups look uninspiring when they're inactive. The groups that work well are those with ten thousand or more members who are all actively engaging. Even those with as many as 1,500 people don't seem to have the following that's needed to stimulate lively conversation. Having said that, I'll be setting up a group shortly. I'm going to trust in the saying 'If you build it, they will come' and see what happens.

MESSENGER: This is a great tool that I use a lot, personally and professionally. It's also good for sending video files that are too large to email. Potential investors regularly contact me on messenger and we end up having long discussions about property and potential investments. While it's great to have public engagement, sometimes it's best to talk privately.

Follow me:
@NicoleSBremner
@EastEightPropertyDevelopment
@LondonCentralDevelopments

## Twitter

Some doomsayers are predicting the beginning of the end for Twitter. Perhaps it is in decline, but it's still a useful platform, even if you only use it to pick up news titbits for your business Facebook page. For me, Twitter's strengths are:

- interesting news items

- discussions and engagement with potential suppliers and the press.

While Facebook seems to be more about business-to-consumer (B2C) engagement, Twitter is more about business-to-business (B2B).

I use Twitter to follow as many interesting people as I can find. I then respond to as many of their tweets as possible with my view or experience to start a conversation. If they respond, you can have more meaningful interactions. Unfortunately, many Twitter profiles are run in an automated way. They just use Hootsuite or something similar to chug out automated tweets without engaging with people. I find these tweeters annoying and soon unfollow them.

Don't be afraid to tweet interesting stuff. Blow your own trumpet at times, or other people's, but don't use Twitter just to broadcast your wins. This gets boring. Come up with a way to get the message across that others can engage with. Rather than saying 'We've been nominated for an International Design and Architecture award', think about tweeting 'What do you think of the latest finalists in the International Design and Architecture Awards? Can you spot our entry?' Add a collage of three or five finalists, including your own, and ask for a discussion.

The best way to flatter those you follow is to retweet their tweets. Don't just hit the retweet button – comment on it. Start a conversation with the tweeter and your followers. Show your support and add your voice to their conversation.

The tough thing on Twitter is that you only start looking credible once you have a couple of thousand followers. It's not easy to get to that level. To get started, follow people who follow tweeters you admire. Have conversations with them and slowly build up. Follow non-property people too. Make yourself multi-dimensional and as interesting as possible to a broad range of people.

I use the Crowdfire app to help with my Twitter administration. Some tweeters will follow you so that you follow them, and then unfollow you. Crowdfire helps to track these people so you can unfollow them unless you find them interesting. It also has a daily tip for how to build followers and find new people. I find it an interesting exercise that takes ten minutes while I'm having breakfast.

Like on Facebook, you can have a business and personal Twitter profile. If I were to start again I'd probably only have a personal profile, with a link to my business in my bio. This takes less work – and you are your business, anyway.

If you do have a separate business profile, treat it in a similar way to your Facebook business page. Engage about macro and micro issues surrounding the areas you develop in and property as a whole.

Follow me:
@NicoleBremner
@E8_Developments
@LC_Developments

## LinkedIn

I haven't used LinkedIn to its full potential. It's a B2B platform but you can use it as B2C depending on who you link with. I'm linked with over 4,500 people but I don't follow them as closely as I do on other platforms. It's good for checking what someone looks like before you meet them in a crowded café! Remember, people can see that you've looked at their profile – so be careful how you cyberstalk your exes.

Used correctly, LinkedIn is a good place to share more in-depth posts focusing on issues around property. Think of it like the *Financial Times*. Write to that level. Present yourself at your most professional.

In mid-January 2017, I posted a picture of four properties we were completing the purchase on by 31 January. My LinkedIn lit up. I had over a thousand link requests in three days and they kept coming for over a week afterwards. That one post had tens of thousands of views and I was inundated with messages. Imagine what would happen if I posted regularly. That's the goal now I can see how powerful LinkedIn can be.

Follow me:
@NicoleBremner

## *Instagram*

Instagram is purely visual. It's the social media platform where you present your most polished self. Beautiful imagery, carefully curated and presented at its best. And don't forget the hashtags.

Hashtags are how you grow your following on Instagram. Tag each post with every relevant thing you can think of. For example, if I were to post a computer-generated image (CGI) of the kitchen at my Harrington Gardens development in Kensington I'd use the following tags:

#kitchen
#kitchendesign
#designerkitchen
#interiors
#interiordesign
#dreamkitchen
#kitchengoals
#CGIs
#Kensington
#property
#propertydeveloper
#propertydevelopment
#propertyinvestor

#propertyinvestment
#propertyforsale

You get the message. Tag everything you can think of relating to that post. That way, people searching for anything from #kitchendesign to #propertyinvestment will see your post and might decide to follow you.

Take time to follow other Instagrammers who you find visually appealing. Comment on their posts and try to engage. I find that there's not as much engagement on this platform as on the others; it's more about presenting yourself at your best. But do try. Everyone loves a compliment.

Repost is a great app that lets you repost other people's Instagram pictures and gives the credit to them. The etiquette is that you should also tag #regram to make sure everyone knows it's not your picture.

I haven't used Instagram to its fullest potential yet because I post a lot of pictures of my children. I'm trying to work out how to deal with this as I attract more followers. Given that what I do is so visual, it's a good tool for business. I'll be focusing on it going forward.

Follow me:

@nsbremner

@E8_Developments

@LC_Developments

## *Snapchat*

You might think of teens sending each other naked selfies when I mention Snapchat, but that was years ago. Snapchat is now the fastest-growing social media platform, with over 150 million active users a day.

It took me quite a while to figure out how to use it. Now I love it and allocate most of my daily social media time to snapping.

Unlike Instagram, think of Snapchat as a glimpse into your life: a day in the life of a property developer. It's unedited, raw and instant. Because the image has a finite life (it's automatically deleted after twenty-four hours), there's no point investing money or too much time into it. Just snap.

There are two parts to Snapchat: messaging and stories. Focus first on the stories. This is where you take pictures (snaps) and videos and load them to My Story. They'll stay there for twenty-four hours. Snap anything that's relevant and that you want your followers to see.

Right now, my story contains a live tour of a beautiful home-design store in Austria. It includes snaps and video: a snap of my hand holding a *glühwein* in a bar, what I'm wearing in the snow that day and some videos of a dance party I went to that evening. Pretty diverse. Some of the content is relevant to property and the rest clearly isn't. But it's showing people who I am and all the elements that make me that.

You can see how many people are viewing each snap in your story. Your followers can't see how many other followers you have or any of the snaps you might get as a result of your story. It's all closed in that way, which is why young people like it – their parents can't cyberstalk them like they can on Facebook and Twitter.

Followers can message you about snaps in your story – or any topic, which can get interesting. No one else can see the snaps and they disappear after a limited time. You can send images to each other, which you can view for anywhere between one and ten seconds before they too disappear. If you want to save an image, you can take a screenshot. Only do this with the sender's permission, as it's bad etiquette to screenshot a snap without permission and the sender gets a notification that you have taken a screenshot.

I only started using Snapchat in October 2016. I changed my photo on Facebook and Twitter to my snapcode – the QR code that is unique for every user – and started snapping. Unlike the other platforms, you can't search for people. You have to know their snapcode to add them. This makes it much harder to find people to follow and for them to follow you.

My experience has been positive so far. Because I haven't found many property people yet, I'm trying to be the first to own Snapchat for property in the UK. I've met three people who have gone on to invest in our crowdfunding and I've met a couple more for coffee.

Because people don't have to use their real names, when someone follows me I always follow them back and send a message thanking them for the add and asking if they work in property. If they reply, I save their reply by pressing and holding the text. They'll know I've saved it, but it helps me remember who they are.

Like all social media platforms, Snapchat is about engage-ment. Watch other snapchatters' stories and comment wher-ever possible. Because no one else can see what you're chat-ting about, my interactions tend to be more open and more personal than those on other platforms. For example, one follower recently asked for my opinion on how he has set up his limited companies for a new purchase. I was able to draw him a rough sketch of how mine are set up and send a snap to him. We discussed his set-up for about ten minutes and I referred him to my accountants. You don't tend to get this level of personal interaction on other platforms, such as Facebook, Instagram and Twitter, because they're public.

I'm really excited about and enjoy Snapchat and I'll be spending a lot of my time on this. Followers tend to check in at least once a day, because the snaps only last twenty-four hours and they don't want to miss them.

Follow me:
@nsbremner

## Pinterest

I was hooked on Pinterest when it first launched in 2010. Finally, I had somewhere to organise recipes, outfits and home ideas. I spent a lot of time putting together some really useful and beautiful boards. But I disregarded it as a business tool, so I'm now trying to make up for lost time.

Pinterest is similar to Instagram in that it's highly visual and it's about presenting you, only better. Gary Vaynerchuck calls it 'the Google of images'. Pinterest is where you go to search for ideas. If my architect asks which marble I'd like in the kitchen, I go to Pinterest and search for 'marble worktops', and voila! – there are thousands of beautiful images of marble in kitchens. If I'm looking for small garden landscape ideas I type in 'small garden landscaping' and instantly I have thousands of ideas.

Now you can see why it's so important to have your own images up there. They can be searched and viewed by the hundred million active Pinterest users. Like Instagram, the key is the tags. People search by tags, so tag everything relevant. Creative titles are also important. Rather than 'White marble kitchen' write something like 'Create a dream kitchen with white Carrara marble countertops'.

I like to have my logo on the images too. It's just a little watermark in the corner so when they are shared widely people can search and find you. Some Pinterest enthusiasts don't like the logos on images though, so perhaps do a mix of with and without on your boards.

Try to follow interesting people related to design, architecture and homes. Hopefully they'll like what you're doing and follow your boards too.

Houzz is similar to Pinterest but with a focus on homes, and it's worth dipping into as well. I'll be spending a bit of time there, so search for me.

Follow me on Pinterest:
@NSBremner

## *YouTube*

I completely forgot about YouTube until I was talking to my eight-year-old son about his grand ambitions to become a YouTube star. Suddenly I realised I'd completely overlooked it. Perhaps that says something about my strategy too.

Video is the way forward. There's no argument about that. Any web designer or search engine optimisation (SEO) specialist will tell you that Google has made video an important factor in search optimisation. Put simply, you must have video on your website.

You can and should go further. Video your projects – before, during and after. Video tours, events and architecture. Today, video is about being prolific not perfect. Your viewers don't expect perfection; they expect to engage with you. Mix hand-held videos from your phone with some professional content and you'll have the full package to engage with people.

I do think it's important to have some professional content to share. It's worth spending between £500 and £2,500 on getting a video producer to film you looking your most polished and professional. Think about doing this at the end of a project when you're showcasing it or when you're speaking at a large event. This shows that you can engage with an audience as well as one to one. Whenever I've spoken at events I've asked for the video. While it wouldn't be right to post the whole video, I can use clips with key nuggets of information for Instagram, YouTube, Facebook and Snapchat. Keep recycling your content.

It's worth devoting time to YouTube, as I do get people contacting me saying they found my videos there. Next, I'm going to focus on creating our own channel on YouTube. Watch this space!

Follow me:
@EastEight

Still don't think you have time to play around with social media? I don't think you have time not to. It's the single biggest way to attract investors and it's free (mostly), so why *not* invest the time? Set aside an hour every day to focus on Facebook, Twitter and LinkedIn. Find people to engage with, join groups and chat with other members. Answer messages and posts and reply to tweets.

If you have some extra time while commuting or watching TV, play around with other platforms, such as Instagram, Pinterest and Snapchat. Ideally, find snappable, Instagrammable and tweetable opportunities throughout your day. In a nice café with great cake? Take a picture and use it. See a great front door? Take a picture. When you have a spare moment you can Instagram it. In a couple of weeks you can then snap it and Pinterest it. You can use your materials across all the platforms.

That said, try to keep some content unique. Don't take a picture of beautiful architecture in Rome and then post it on Twitter, Snapchat, Instagram, Facebook and Pinterest at the same time. If you do, people won't follow you on all the platforms. Post one immediately and save the others for another time.

There are other social media platforms that I haven't mentioned. This isn't to say that Reddit, Tumblr and Medium, for example, aren't important. In this book I've focused on the biggest ones, but Tumblr, for example, has over 555 million users so it's worth looking at.

Here's a link to an interactive chart by Statista showing the top social networks ranked by users.[8]

What I find hardest to manage about all these platforms is direct messages. I struggle to stay on top of Facebook messages in posts and messenger and direct messages on Twitter,

---

8  https://www.statista.com/statistics/272014/global-social-networks-ranked-by-number-of-users/

LinkedIn, Instagram, Snapchat and Pinterest. I'll recall that I had a message from someone asking for something, but I can't remember which platform it was on. Add WhatsApp, email and text messages and I'm lost. I use a BlackBerry, which lets me keep all communications from these (except Snapchat) in one place, and this helps. To stay on top of it all, set aside some time each day to review each platform and answer questions there and then. If you can't, note the platform and the task in your project management tool and respond when you can. Better still, outsource the communication when you can. Often, it's not something you need to respond to yourself.

At the end of each project I hire a professional photographer to come in and take dozens of pictures. It's great for the business portfolio and gives us heaps of material we can use on Pinterest and across the other social media platforms – not to mention in marketing materials and on the website. It's well worth the outlay of £500 to £1,500 for beautiful pictures that you can use time and time again.

This might seem daunting, but it's important to build your personal and business brand. When you start, it will soon become second nature and you'll find your authentic voice. Just do it.

If you're serious about building your brand, consider attending a workshop by Shaa Wasmund. She runs the successful

Freedom Collective on Facebook and holds regular events in London. If you really want to commit, look at the Key Person of Influence programme by Daniel Priestley of Dent Global. It's a six-month programme that will take you through the steps of building a modern business. For a more personalised programme tailored to property, contact us at learn@ east-eight.com.

# Summary

- Three key factors for growing your property business are:

    - carefully chosen joint ventures

    - crowdfunding and

    - building your brand.

- Choose joint venture partners wisely. Do you really want to work with this person for the next year or more?

- Be open and honest at every step of the way. Hiding things will only cause problems later.

- Never fall foul of PS13/3. If in doubt, don't discuss investment. You can explain what you do and let the potential investor come to their own conclusion about working with you.

- Consider investing in a development. You'll not only

be able to make some money but also learn about the property development process. A good developer will be open with you, allowing you to learn along the way.

• Build your brand. Your logo and name should reflect your values and vision. Incorporate this into a website and across social media.

• Start speaking. Start with smaller property meetings to practise your story and work your way up to the larger ones. It's the most efficient and effective way to reach hundreds of people.

• Get on all the major social media platforms. Engage with people. Remember that it's about being prolific not perfect.

# The Property Process

## Strategies

Perhaps by now you've decided that property is definitely for you. You're just not sure of the process or how to start. There's so much jargon; so many strategies touted by experts all vying to take your money to teach you how to reach financial freedom. By charging anything from £300 to £30,000 (yes, that's right) they sell you the dream.

Thankfully I didn't realise any of these experts existed when I started out as an accidental landlord or even when I first started developing. It wasn't until I thought, 'Hey, property is great, all my mummy friends should do it' and started looking at courses that I stumbled upon Property Tribes and was introduced to the world of property education – the good, the bad and the ugly.

How do you choose a strategy? For me it was straightforward. I knew I didn't like dealing with tenants. I'd enjoyed the process of developing my own home and working with my builders. I also had a bit of cash saved. As I wanted my money to work hard and I didn't need an income, development was the perfect option.

The most important factor in deciding which strategy you'll embark upon is cash. More specifically, your need for it and how much you have available. Do you need a regular income? If so, consider an income-producing strategy, such as buy-to-let. Can't manage your property full-time? Have it managed. Want to be fully hands-on? Perhaps an HMO is the right strategy for you. Buy-to-sell was the obvious choice for me. I didn't come to this realisation straight away, though. In fact, I nearly didn't work in property at all.

If you've decided on development but you're not familiar with the right end of a hammer, you'll need builders and probably a project manager. Don't have time to be active? Consider investing with a partner who'll run the project for you. If you don't have a large pot to invest and you're not a sophisticated and high net worth investor, think about crowdfunding, especially if the developers will let you learn while you invest.

The list of strategies is endless, but I've set out the main ones in the table below:

| Strategy | Summary |
| --- | --- |
| Buy-to-let | Buying a property to let it out to a tenant. |
| | It can be relatively easy to get a buy-to-let mortgage if you meet the lender requirements. It generates a regular income if you have good tenants. However, you will need to manage tenants at some level, and recent changes mean that it might not be as profitable for many investors. |
| Buy-to-sell | Buying a property to add value and sell for a profit. The property might need just a paint or a loft extension. But the end goal is the same – to sell for a profit. |
| Holiday lets, including Airbnb | Buying a property to let for shorter periods in tourist areas. There is a high turnover of tenants and more administration in exchange for a higher income. Airbnb has become a standalone strategy for many investors. |

| Strategy | Summary |
|---|---|
| HMOS | Houses of multiple occupation. Renting out a property to at least three people who are not part of one family. It can bring in more income from rent than if you were to rent out the property as a whole. It is regulated in some areas. |
| Assisted sales | Working with the owner of a property to renovate or develop their property in exchange for a share of the profits. See my story on this later in this chapter. |
| Flipping | Another term for buy-to-sell but often used for buying off-plan, prior to the completion, and sometimes even start, of the build, and selling the property on without carrying out much, if any, work on it. |
| Lease options | Leasing a property with the option to buy it for a set price at the end of a set rental period. This can bring in more rent for you while allowing the leaseholder to secure a lower price now in a rising market. |
| Student lets | Similar to HMOs, but renting to students for an academic year. These properties need to be close to universities and usually attract a higher rental income. Some larger developers are now building specialist student accommodation and pre-letting the whole building to universities for a set period. |

| Strategy | Summary |
| --- | --- |
| Rent-to-rent | Leasing a property and then renting it out on a room-by-room basis to maximise the rental income. |
| Planning gain | Buying a property without planning permission or which has been under-planned (where the building might be further extended for example) and selling it once the planning permission has been granted. This lets you profit from the extra value the planning permission brings to the property. |
| Serviced accommodation | Similar to holiday lets, but with more hotel-type services, such as housekeeping. |
| Off-plan purchase | Buying properties off-plan and taking advantage of the discount sometimes offered by developers. |
| No money down, other people's money | Convincing someone with money to lend it to you so that you can carry out any of these property strategies in exchange for a percentage of the profits. This strategy requires a track record to attract investment. It sounds attractive but it can be difficult to attract the level of investment you need to make enough income if you don't have much experience. |

| Strategy | Summary |
|---|---|
| Private rental sector and build-to-rent | Building American-style condominium developments where the plan from the outset is to rent all the apartments. These are a more recent strategy in the UK and are mostly used by medium to large developers. |
| Microflats | Convincing the planning department that the demand for self-contained flats in the area is large enough for you to carve up a property into smaller units than permitted under the London Supplementary Planning Documents. It can be highly profitable, as you have a larger number of units in a development and can charge higher rent. |

You can use joint ventures as part of any of these strategies. (See Chapter Three for more on joint ventures.)

In this section, we'll look at some of these strategies in more detail.

## Buy-to-Let

One of the most popular strategies is buy-to-let. The advantages are that it can be relatively easy to get a buy-to-let mortgage if you meet the lender requirements and it generates a regular income if you have good tenants. The disadvantages are that you might not have good tenants and even if you have managing agents you will need to manage tenants on some level. Also, the recent s24 changes mean that this strategy might not be as profitable for many investors in future.

This is a relatively new strategy, with the first buy-to-let mortgages only introduced in 1996. You might meet a few long-term investors who have been doing this for thirty years or more, but mortgages weren't available for this back then.

It didn't take long for the buy-to-let market to go crazy. I won't go into the full history, as there are plenty of books on the subject. But banks were doling out 110% mortgages to anyone who could self-certify an income. Thousands of new landlords jumped on the bandwagon and were soon building up mega-portfolios with little of their own money invested.

Two of the most famous landlords, for many reasons, are Fergus and Judith Wilson.[9] It's reported that they own around one thousand buy-to-let properties, mostly around Ashford and Maidstone in Kent. They come in at number 453 on the *Sunday Times* rich list with a fortune of about £180 million.

The former maths teachers started buying in their own names

---

9  For more information, see the entry in Wikipedia: https://en .wikipedia.org/wiki/Fergus_and_Judith_Wilson.

in the 1990s. This came to an abrupt halt with the global financial crisis in 2008, when it was reported that they were in arrears on their mortgage payments by about £350,000. The Wilsons got off lightly and survived to restructure their portfolio. Others weren't so lucky.

According to an article in the *Independent*,[10] in 2009 over three hundred and fifty people a day were becoming insolvent, with record numbers of businesses collapsing throughout 2008 and 2009. Many of these were landlords tied up with banks that were recalling loans.

As I mentioned earlier, I don't think the banks acted responsibly during this period. They often called in loans because of the hype around potential concerns. If the banks had given the developers time to continue with construction and let them refinance so they could hold the project until the markets turned, the personal and professional outcomes would have been better for so many.

Some developers who went bankrupt have gone on to bigger and better things, but the pain at the time must have been intense. I never want to go through this. My biggest fear is having to tell my children that mummy lost their home. I prefer to keep my loan-to-value rates at a conservative level

---

10  http://www.independent.co.uk/news/uk/home-news/record-nu mbers-are-declared-bankrupt-as-recession-bites-1570698.html

of around 50% across my portfolio. This way, if the worst should happen I can sell a property quickly and still, hopefully, cover the loan.

Interestingly, it was during this period that Avi was forced to start his own in-house construction company. He was working on an iconic church on Abbey Road in St. John's Wood, not far from the famous Beatles crossing. The bank had insisted that he work with a top-name building contractor. Partway into the project the contractor declared bankruptcy, taking millions of pounds of developer funds with them. The bank then insisted on another top contractor. Unfortunately, it wasn't long before they also declared bankruptcy. Left with no choice, Avi hired an experienced project manager and put together his own team. While it was difficult at the time, it was one of his best decisions he's made. It now allows us to develop in a cost-effective way without factoring in a contractor profit.

The high loan-to-value strategy doesn't work anymore, due to tax changes announced and bitterly fought against during 2016. These changes restrict the income tax relief that landlords can claim on residential property finance costs to just the basic rate of tax. Rolling out from April 2017, these changes could have huge implications for current landlords' holdings. We're yet to see the full extent of the effect on property prices and the buy-to-let strategy as a whole. If you're considering a buy-to-let strategy, please do an online search or see this discussion on Property Tribes.[11]

## Buy-to-Sell

My decision to use a buy-to-sell strategy was an easy one. I didn't like dealing with tenants and I didn't need a regular income. I didn't want to keep hold of an asset. I just wanted to refurbish and sell it. That was the strategy in the beginning, and it worked well for me while the market was rising. Once the market slowed it was harder to make returns that compensated for not only the outlay but also the risk and my time.

Once you've made the decision to buy-to-sell, the next step is to determine the level of return you're willing to accept. This return needs to cover your costs, but it should also reflect the riskiness of the investment and pay you for your time. For me, there was never any point in investing to take just a salary. Why invest £250,000 and borrow another £250,000 to earn a £30,000 return? I'd rather go and get a job for £30,000 a year, without any risks, and invest the £250,000 in something that would bring me a higher return. Much safer.

---

11 http://www.propertytribes.com/government-sets-out-s ection-24-roll-out-t-127625811.html.

In my opinion, too many developers are taking on lower value properties. In early 2016 I was trying to buy a property in Hackney Wick near the Fashion Hub area (who saw that coming?). I submitted an offer of about £5.1 million, just over the asking price of £5 million. I heard nothing in return. It was off the market, so I assumed that the vendor had decided not to sell.

In December 2016 one of my regular investors forwarded an email about an investment opportunity. It was the same property. When I looked at the details I saw they'd paid £7.1 million. No wonder my offer was ignored. The numbers were even more interesting. The total debt was about £8 million, the total costs just under £9 million and the expected profit was £1.5 million: a profit on costs of under 17%. And their sales prices were optimistic too. It was clear that no one was going to make money on this deal except the lenders.

Why accept this level of risk? The developer was putting in £450,000. He'd be better off taking on a much smaller project with that equity and accepting a bigger chunk of a smaller profit. It makes me nervous when developers push up prices with optimistic valuations. These are the developers who crumble with the slightest increase in interest rates, because they don't have the cash to cover interest rate payments if they overrun and the bank calls them in. Unfortunately, this can bring down the market for those who are more prudent.

Knowing when to walk away from a deal is the best lesson a developer can learn. As Avi says to me when I'm disappointed about missing out, it's better to regret the deals you missed than the ones you bought. It may be painful at the time, but it's better to walk away than overpay and turn your dream into a nightmare.

## Airbnb

Airbnb has become a disruptive force within the short-let and holiday-let sectors. Some landlords, known as hosts, rely completely on Airbnb as a strategy, buying their properties just to let them for a short time. In most cases, short lets fall foul of leasehold contracts, mortgage agreements, insurance policies and planning laws.

Buckling under pressure from local authorities in the UK, from Spring 2017 Airbnb will limit hosts to renting out their property for 90 days a year or fewer. This will be a huge blow to hosts who rely on this business. They'll have to seek other providers, such as One Fine Stay, to fill the void. None of the other players have the reach that Airbnb does. It will be interesting to see if people find a way to work around this.

I've used Airbnb as a strategy for a couple of years now. It's the perfect way for me to fill a property for a short period while I'm waiting for planning permission or if sales are slow. Englefield Road is a good example. The works finished in summer 2015 but I didn't sell it until Autumn later that year. I didn't want this expensive asset to sit empty from a security or cash-flow perspective, so I put it on Airbnb. Because it was a beautiful and large property, I had no problems keeping it fully booked.

A large global accounting firm rented it for a week for a team-building event. Then a prominent Nigerian politician rented it for a couple of months. It was great for finding out about snags. For example, I found out that the blinds didn't work properly. There was some damage, but it was cosmetic and nothing that £1,000 couldn't fix; the tenants paid.

One neighbour constantly complained about the noise of the tenants. I took it seriously until she started to complain when it was empty...

When I first bought Harrington Gardens I put that on Airbnb too. Being near South Kensington tube station meant it was always booked. All was well until we received a polite but firm call from the building's managing agent. The woman who lived downstairs had requested that we cease the short lets, as it was a security issue. The agent reminded me that it was against the terms of the lease. We immediately complied and took the property off Airbnb.

More recently, I've been using Airbnb for a flat in Hackney while I'm selling it. I keep the price low to focus on regular income rather than maximising profit. I also have a five-day minimum stay so I don't need to constantly send in cleaners. It's fully booked and generates income that I wouldn't have otherwise. None of the other leaseholders in the building mind. One Airbnb guest even enquired about buying the property. Sadly, she didn't have the funds.

With the change in the regulations, I believe the Airbnb market will change. As such, I haven't included a how-to Airbnb for developers in this book. If you'd be interested in having information to download, please let me know: contact@east-eight.com.

## HMOS

HMOS has been the buzzword of the last five years. The promise of packing them full and collecting higher rents has enticed many landlords and new property investors into the sometimes shady world of multiple occupancy. There's nothing new about HMOS, or bedsits as they were once known – they've just become a strategy. Watch any period drama and you'll see an often elderly widow renting rooms with a washstand and otherwise shared facilities to young professional men.

My experience with tenants put me off an HMO strategy. The thought of multiple tenants in one property all calling because they can't work the white goods fills me with dread. It's also harder to secure lending, although the lending market is catching up. Although I didn't know it at the time, my first three properties were HMO-to-house conversions. I've reversed the trend in areas where HMOs no longer worked as a strategy.

## Assisted Sales

Buying a property outright is cash-intensive. How do you get started if you don't have a large pot of savings? There are courses out there about using other people's money. But would you really give a significant amount of money to someone with no record in property development with the hope of turning a profit? I certainly wouldn't. I believe the only people making money on this type of strategy are the ones who are selling the courses. The hard reality? It rarely happens.

Another option for those with little cash is assisted sales. Rather than buy the property, you can work with the owners to either renovate or develop it. You then split the profits on a pre-agreed ratio. Again, I'm not sure why someone would trust a complete beginner to manage their property refurbishment. But if you have a relative who wants to help you get started, or you are an architect, interior designer with some exposure to property, it can be a good way to learn.

Just as I accidentally became a landlord, I assisted a friend with their sale before I even knew there was a term for it. I've known Lily and John (names changed) since 2006. They had owned their flat in south-east London for about fifteen years. Unfortunately, the property was flooded when the drains overflowed. This caused major damage to the basement flat of this Georgian listed building.

Further disaster struck Lily and John and they needed to use the insurance payment to help a family member. When I visited, they were living in a cold, damp basement flat without any flooring or properly functioning bathrooms. To top it off, they were in a dispute with the neighbour above over issues surrounding the flooding and outstanding payments.

Lily and John wanted to sell up, pay up and move on with their lives in another part of the country. They'd accepted an offer from a local buyer, but after months in the conveyancing process the buyer dropped out. At first I thought I could buy the flat and renovate it. But then the stamp duty rates increased and it was no longer feasible. I proposed what I now know is an assisted sale: I would completely renovate the flat, relocate Lily and John and pay their rent in exchange for half of any uplift in the property value at the time of the sale.

I decided to do it as a joint venture with my builder. He could meet the build costs while I focused on the loans and the rent and relocation costs.

Just a couple of weeks into the renovation, the problematic neighbour complained to the council about the works. As the building was grade II listed, an enforcement officer came to the site and shut it down immediately. Having renovated a grade II listed building before, I knew the council was taking a heavy-handed approach for a simple cosmetic refurbishment. The neighbour had exaggerated the extent of the project, claiming that we were doing structural work.

During the three months we had to down tools, Lily and John's financial situation worsened and we had to look at other options. Auctioning the property seemed to be the best way to secure a quick sale while the flat looked like a building site. At the time, some experts were selling courses on making more money from properties by making them look like they were derelict. We hoped we could capitalise on this idea too.

Foxtons had valued the flat at £780,000 before the work, when the market was buoyant in Spring 2013. Given that the market had cooled and it looked like a building site we placed the reserve at £580,000 with a guide price of £599,000. There was plenty of interest, with dozens of people passing through on the open days.

With butterflies in my stomach, I attended the auction. I watched with disappointment as the price reached £572,000 – £8,000 shy of the reserve – before going unsold. That phone call to Lily and John was a difficult one. We decided to press on with the refurbishment as soon as the planning application was accepted. It was a blow.

Thankfully the local authority could see that nothing untoward was going on with the renovation and allowed us to continue. We finished the project and put the light, airy, modernised flat on the market for £730,000. I won't go into the details, as that would be a book in itself, but we ended up getting close to exchange with first one buyer and then another who both dropped out. We finally found a motivated buyer. But the troublesome (and troubled) neighbour asserted himself again and attempted to block the process by stalling on the lease extension. I still don't know how he did it, but finally John managed to negotiate an agreement with the neighbour and the sale exchanged and completed just before Christmas in 2016.

The whole process had taken nearly two years and I made a net profit of about £20,000 on total loans of £116,000. It hardly warranted the stress, management and time I'd put in. I'm glad I did it because it helped a friend, but it was hardly a route to riches.

# How to Choose a Strategy

The strategy you decide to follow will determine how you take your business forward. It's important to get it right from the outset. You can change it, but it's not easy – even the structure for tax purposes is determined by your strategy.

What to consider:

- **TIME**  What does your work week look like? What would you like your work week to look like? Can you commit to this full-time or is it a part-time venture?

- **CASH**  Do you have any? Do you need regular income to support yourself and family? If you have a lump sum, you can consider buying to sell or developing. If you need regular income, you'll need that rental payment each month.

- **EXISTING SKILLS**  If you're already skilled in a trade, you're starting from a great position. While you might not want to get your hands dirty any more, you'll certainly know if a job is being done right or if quotes are accurate. Previous financial, branding, marketing and social media skills are just as important. Carrying out the work is just one side to the business. Building a big brand that people want to work with takes some marketing expertise. If you don't have these skills, do some courses, hire people and talk to people.

Remember, you don't have to stick to one strategy. You can add more and mix them up. For example, you might have a buy-to-let portfolio and develop a couple of properties a year, giving you income and capital growth.

My strategy has been to stick with developing. I'm hands-on, I want to work full-time and I have the cash to invest large sums into each project. I don't rely on a regular income from property so I can afford to sit on one- or two-year projects with a view to making a larger gain at the end.

I'm looking at building blocks of flats to rent, which I'll hold for income. Having economies of scale and someone else to manage the block is the only way a lettings strategy will work for me. Decide what works for you and then just do it.

# Structure

Once you've decided on your strategy, before you do anything else you must see a specialist property accountant. I can't stress this enough. The way you structure your activities could make the difference between a big profit and a big tax bill.

When I decided to go into property, Michael wanted advice from our accountant. He had looked after our personal accounts for the past couple of years so we thought he was the best person to advise on how to structure our first foray into bricks and mortar.

I had a one-hour call with our accountant, discussing source of funds, strategy and how I envisaged it would work on a day-to-day basis. Two weeks later I received a report echoing everything we had discussed. The conclusion was that I needed to seek the advice of a specialist property accountant, because ours wasn't familiar with property as an investment class. Then I nearly fell off my chair – included in the email was an invoice for about £6,000!

Thankfully I met a specialist property tax and management accounting firm. For significantly less than £6,000 they advised me on the best structure for our personal situation and goals.

My accountant's advice was to set up a holding company. This would be a limited company. Each new property would be purchased through a special purpose vehicle (SPV). An SPV is a company incorporated especially for the purchase of a property. It is fully owned by our holding company. I personally would loan the start-up capital to the holding company. The holding company would, in turn, loan it to each SPV to buy each property. The SPV is active while the project is underway and, at the end, the post-tax profits are distributed to the shareholders (in my case, the holding company) and then the SPV is dissolved.

There are pros and cons of an SPV set-up. The benefits are that if you're a higher-rate taxpayer you can minimise tax by paying the company tax rather than your personal rate. If you keep the profits in the holding company you won't need to pay any personal tax on this money. You can keep the funds to buy more property.

If you're looking to buy a property that is held in a company, you can save a small fortune in stamp duty land tax if you buy the company rather than the property. This is a more advanced strategy, so take professional advice.

The downside to SPVs is that the finance costs can be higher than if you borrow in your own name. There's really no way around this. If you're used to personal mortgage rates or buy-to-let mortgage rates, development rates are frightening. This is just the price you have to pay for the tax savings.

Everyone's situation is unique and regulations change all the time, so please don't just follow what I have done. This is merely an illustration and what was best for me at the time. Find a trusted accountant and set your business up the right way for you from the outset.

# Finance

When I first started in property I didn't realise that any type of bank lending was available for small developers like me. I knew about buy-to-let mortgages, but because I was carrying out extensive renovations I knew I wouldn't qualify. Instead, I used cash to buy the first couple of properties. But, of course, not everyone has £1.2 million in cash available to them.

The issue with using cash, especially if you don't have an endless pot of gold, is that you go through peaks and troughs. This makes it hard to smooth out your income. One day you're rolling in cash and ready to buy. Then you complete the sale and renovate the property. By the end, you're skint because you've spent the budget, plus some more. We've all seen it on *Grand Designs* and *Homes Under The Hammer*. Everyone goes over budget.

While you're cash-poor, you can't buy another property because you need to wait for the previous property to sell. It can take two years to turn over one property and move on to the next. It all depends on how quickly you can buy, renovate and sell the first property and then buy the next.

Michael smiles when I complain about my workload. He says that the plan was that I do one or two properties a year, buying with cash and slowly building up my capital. I wasn't patient enough for that. If you're content with slow and steady growth, good for you – it's safer. Continue to use cash and you'll have a comfortable experience and sleep more deeply than I do. But if you want to scale up more quickly, you'll need to use some sort of debt and perhaps some equity as well.

There are two options for finance. One is equity and the other is debt.

## Equity

Equity is the value of an asset less the debt. It's also the amount of money you want to put into a project or that the lender requires you to put in. Most lenders ask you to put in at least some equity, although some will lend 100% for a larger chunk of the profit. More on those later.

For my first couple of projects I put in all the equity. The benefits are that you're completely in control of the project. You don't have to keep an investor or bank informed or have them breathing down your neck if things don't go exactly to plan.

The downside is the inability to scale up as quickly because of the time it takes to turn properties around, as discussed above. It also means that your cash-on-cash returns (how much cash you receive back divided by the cash you invest) are lower. Let's assume you buy a property for £100,000 and sell it for £120,000. See the difference in your returns based on how much equity you invest:

| | | |
|---|---|---|
| Purchase price | 100,000 | 100,000 |
| Equity | 100,000 | 50,000 |
| Debt | 0 | 50,000 |
| Sales price | 120,000 | 120,000 |
| **Profit** | **20,000** | **20,000** |
| **Cash-on-cash return** | **20%** | **40%** |

By having a prudent level of borrowing on a project, you can invest in more than one property at a time and double your cash return.

The biggest question you need to ask yourself is what level of equity you're comfortable with. To put it another way, what level of *borrowing* are you comfortable with? I prefer to keep the total borrowing in my portfolio to around 50%. At that level, I believe that I can repay the debt if the bank calls in the loan and I can cover the interest payments if necessary.

If you're comfortable with lower levels of equity and higher levels of borrowing, there are lenders out there for you. One lender requires the developer to put in only 10% of the equity.

The lender will put up the remaining funds and then take 70% of the profits.

If I'm going to find the property, structure the deal, run the whole project and manage the sale, I won't be happy with 30% of the returns. But if you only have to put up 10% of the funds, it could be a good way to get started.

Friends and family might also help if you need a short-term loan to cover your cash requirements between one property purchase and the next. When I started speaking to friends about what I was doing and my successes, many wanted to get involved.

While Rob (name changed) was visiting from abroad, we discussed my first property development, Lenthall Road. I explained my frustration that I couldn't buy another property. The sale had been agreed but we hadn't yet exchanged so I couldn't make an offer on another property I'd found in Parkholme Road.

Rob analysed my Lenthall project and the potential numbers on Parkholme and decided he wanted to be part of it. To secure the purchase of Parkholme, Rob put up all the initial equity for the purchase £1.5 million plus some funds for the initial works and we started the demolition. Once my sale of Lenthall had completed I repaid Rob the balance. That made us 50/50 shareholders. Once the project finished we split the profits 50/50. While I undertook the management of the project, we still split the profits proportionately in recognition of him putting up all the funds for a couple of months.

Parkholme Road was actually one of my failures. It only returned 13%, which was disappointing. One reason for this was that we had fully financed the project with cash: some £1.9 million in the end. The other reason was the change in stamp duty, which made luxury property even more expensive.

Had we borrowed 50% of the required funds the return would have been over 30% and I wouldn't consider it a fail.

Another reason I believe I failed at Parkholme was the time it took to sell and the fact that I didn't accept a good offer I received early in the sales process.

I finished the renovation of the property in June 2015. The finish was beautiful and it was a large property of over 2,770 square feet. I felt confident that it would sell. Two local agents valued it at £2.7 million. We were set to make a profit of about £600,000 after costs.

Early in the process the agent called and said he had a prospective buyer who had been looking in the area for a while.

He had viewed the property before I bought it and decided it was too much work for him.

So I let in the estate agent and went to sit in my car while the agent waited for his buyer. I noticed this scruffy-looking guy walking up the street wearing shorts, a baseball cap and a rucksack. I thought the agent had invited an unemployed friend just to show he was being proactive. The scruffy man entered my house and spent the next twenty minutes viewing. The agent then came out to my car and said that his client wanted to meet me.

Out came Mr Scruffy and shook my hand. My jaw dropped as I realised I was shaking hands with a very famous actor from a US sitcom! I tried to play it cool and forgot to remove my sunglasses. I guess that's quite LA showbiz, though. The actor was complimentary about the work I had done and thanked me for my time. He asked if he could return later that day with his wife to see the property.

A couple of days later an offer came through of £2.4 million cash with a quick exchange and completion. Hindsight is golden, as they say, and really I should have snapped up the offer. Instead I said, 'thank you but no thank you'. And the actor went away, never to be heard from again. Well, not by me, anyway. He did perform in a play in the West End later that summer.

In the end, I sold the property months later for £2.2 million to the head of UK operations for a large social network. I was so sure I'd get £2.6 million for the property. But in the end it was better to sell, make a smaller return and reinvest the cash than to wait for the right buyer at a more palatable price.

The difficulty in this experience was communicating my failure to Rob. Communication is the most important thing in any investor/developer relationship. Keep the dialogue frequent and transparent in good times and bad. Warn the investor about any changes to the plan, especially of any risks. Rob wasn't thrilled, but he had tracked the changes in the market and because I'd kept him up to date he wasn't surprised and could take it on board. It would have been worse to keep him in the dark about changes and then surprise him at the end when dividing up the profit.

# Debt

The whole process of raising debt is my least favourite part of property development. I have so many horror stories that I'm not sure which ones to start with. If you'll allow me a rant, I believe the system is broken. Perhaps it's the cautious state of the economy or the changes implemented after the crisis in 2008. But raising debt is the single most stressful part of my job and it's one I could really do without.

I could mention a number of near misses with lenders unable to meet deadlines, but that would lower the tone. Now, from experience, I never like to be left in a situation where I'm exposed to a default. Always make sure your debt is arranged well in advance and there is cash available if the worst should happen and a lender fails to meet a completion deadline.

## Types of Debt

There are many types of debt and many types of debt providers, depending on the situation and your requirements. If you're buying a development opportunity without planning permission, you'll need to go down the bridging finance route.

I was horrified at the thought of bridging when I first started out. The rates are around 1% a month. It seems extortionate to me. As I moaned to a seasoned property professional, she told me it's just the way you have to buy if you want the deal. It still makes my eyes water.

Bridging is exactly that – a bridge between buying the property and getting a development loan or making a sale. Once planning permission is in place or you have a tenant, you can switch to a development loan or a buy-to-let mortgage.

Some developers try to get away with using a regular buy-to-let mortgage. This is risky, as it contravenes the terms of a buy-to-let mortgage, and I wouldn't take that chance. Think longer term: it's better to build a relationship with a lender so you can be sure they'll back you if you bring them a good project.

Bridging lenders will offer up to around 75% loan-to-value on a bridge for a term of up to twelve months. This varies depending on the lender. High street banks don't usually offer bridges. It's more specialised lending companies or private lenders who want to make money from lending their surplus out.

I prefer to work with private lenders. These are individuals who have a few million pounds that they lend to a handful of select developers. They focus on a long-term mutually beneficial relationship. They're more flexible on terms, they're quicker and I can build a direct relationship with the principals. Most will still need a valuation (the bane of my property existence) but they're prepared to take a pragmatic view on the results based on your record.

Development lending is available once your planning permission is in place. High street banks are the most competitive, but they can be arduous to deal with because of the hoops they have to jump through for regulatory purposes. The competitive rates I am offered by my bank reflect my experience and the long-standing relationship.

A development loan can cover up to 100% of development costs. This means you don't have to dip into your own pocket – unless you go over budget. Usually, the lender will contract a monitoring surveyor who, for a fee, will monitor the project at set periods. The surveyor has to sign off on progress before the bank issues each tranche of the loan.

For my first development loan with a high street bank, they didn't want a monitoring surveyor, because the project was too small at £330,000. Instead, the bank insisted that I pay all the suppliers and employees by cheque. They could then monitor the cheques I wrote and approve payment. My subcontractors were not happy about working from 8am to 5pm, Monday to Friday and from 8am to 1pm on Saturdays and then having to bank cheques. My bookkeeper would run around all the banks on a Monday depositing the cheques for the guys. It was a tedious experience, but we got into the groove eventually.

A slightly newer concept is that of crowdfunding debt. There are some options out there but the market is not sufficiently mature enough to rely upon. I'm currently looking at all options. For example, one crowdfunding platform is relaunching with the ability to take ISA funds. I need to wait and see if it's possible to raise the levels of debt required for the size of the projects we're working on but it could be an interesting option.

# Brokers

You can go direct to lenders, but this is a minefield. There are so many options. I prefer to have a broker sort through the various offers and present the best couple for each scenario. Additionally, if a loan falls through a broker can make sure there are one or two backups. The time it would take for me to sort through all of this is worth more than a regular broker fee. And often the lender pays the fee.

Like lenders, there are various levels of broker. Ask for recommendations and go with a professional with a good record and an enthusiastic approach.

# Purchase

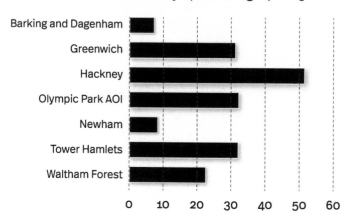

House Price Growth in the Olympic Boroughs, 2005–2012

## Where to Buy

Deciding to buy your first investment property is equally exciting and nerve-racking. Where to buy your first property is an important decision. The reason I first invested in Hackney is because I don't like commuting. I love to walk everywhere and I wanted to walk to my site each day. I also knew Hackney really well. I knew most of the streets, the houses that were being developed and the ones that needed refurbishing. If an agent sent details of a property through I could act quickly, because I knew where it was.

I recommend sticking to one area at first – preferably your local area. This is the place you spend most of your time and you can get to the site quickly if you have to make a speedy decision. It's easy to get lost in the number of potential deals. By reducing your search area, you focus your search. You can quickly rule out properties that fall outside your area.

Before I made my first purchase I spent months tracking all the properties for sale in the E8 area of London. I set up a spreadsheet and entered data on every property I viewed: the asking price, square feet, price per square foot and notes on the condition. With all this data available I could quickly see if a property came on the market that was significantly undervalued relative to other properties. I'd keep in touch with the agent and find out how much properties sold for before the information became public on the Land Registry. This data was so valuable for my analysis. It was an invaluable lesson from my banking days.

## How to Find Property

The traditional way to find a property is through an estate agent. Get to know all the local ones. Go into their offices so you're not just another voice on the phone. Tell the agent what you're looking for, the exact area, the budget and how quickly you're able to move. Drop in a development CV or company brochure too. This shows the agent you're serious and puts you at the top of their list if something new comes in.

At times, estate agents get properties that need to be marketed quietly or quickly. If the agent knows you can move quickly, you'll be one of the first people they tell. Sometimes I was the only one to be told about a deal because the agent knew I could perform and that I would pay the required price.

People are springing up all over the place calling themselves sourcers. The very name makes me bristle. After a bad experience with one on a recent deal, I no longer work with them. You can be sure that nine times out of ten the property they're pushing is on the open market. If it's not, the seller is chancing – putting the property on with a sourcer for an inflated price in the hope that they'll get it. I've seen this time and time again.

Another sourcing trick is to repackage properties that are listed with a large agent, often without any financials, and pass it off as being off the market. This is how I was caught out by a sourcer. I learned the hard way and I would warn you not to work with them. The exception is if you employ someone to search for a property for you. Avi and I did this with Harrington Gardens.

Ross (name changed) is a young guy who has known Avi

for a few years. He's enthusiastic and wants to progress in property. Ross brought Harrington Gardens to our attention. He then dug up all the comparable price and sales data and issues surrounding the short lease.

We offered Ross a percentage of either the purchase price or the sales price. He intelligently chose the sales price and is now assisting in the project management of the site. Ross will not only profit from sourcing this project but also learn about the development side. Find ambitious people like this to work with, as they can assist you as you scale up your business.

Auctions are another place to find property. In recent years, I've stayed away, as it became more expensive to buy at auction than to buy on the market. The adrenaline in the room spurs people on to overbid. During the peak of 2012–2014, the prices were ridiculous.

Now that prices are softening, auctions might be worth another look. What's great is that an auction contract is binding. Once the hammer goes down you pay the deposit and you have to complete the sale or purchase. There's a level of certainty and speed that you don't have with a traditional sale or purchase.

# Submitting an Offer

You've narrowed down an area and found an undervalued property that's ripe for renovation. Now you must make an offer. The offer needs to include a price, of course. It also needs to include the period to exchange and completion, and whether or not your offer is cash or dependent on finance.

A pet peeve is that every developer will submit a 'cash' offer even if they don't have cash. Be honest. If you don't have cash, don't submit a cash offer. Tell them you have access to quick finance.

I like to submit my offer informally over the phone with the agent first. He or she might be able to guide me immediately. This is where trust is so important. I don't deal with agents who I believe are lying to try to push up the price.

I'll say something like 'I'm considering submitting an offer for £950,000. How will this appeal to the vendor?' From their response, I'll be able to gauge the likelihood of success. They'll say outright if it will fly or not. If they say 'Yes, let's see how it goes', I know it's a good one. If they tell me that it's been offered before but rejected, I'll dig a little deeper to find out why. Perhaps I can improve the terms of the offer without increasing the price.

If the other offer is dependent on finance and I have cash, that could be more acceptable. I might want to offer a £10,000 non-refundable deposit to secure the property and show my commitment to buy. I might say that I'll guarantee exchange within a set period of time with a quick completion too. All these things can help you secure the property without increasing the price.

In a soft market, you might not need to add any sweeteners because there's no demand. Judge the situation from your local intelligence and the feedback you're getting from the agent and make an informed decision. I find that the better the property, the quicker you'll need to act to secure it and the more sweeteners you'll need to add to the deal.

Once you've bounced your offer off the agent, you'll need to send it in writing. I like to write a formal email that clearly outlines my offer price and full details. It also contains my solicitor's contact details, my development CV and a copy of my proof of funds. Make it easy for the agent to make your offer look good. Be prepared to negotiate, though. No vendor should accept your first offer unless it's a best and final offers situation.

# Conveyancing

Your offer has been accepted. Congratulations! But keep the champagne on ice. It's not a done deal yet. The next step is to get the contracts to your solicitor. Your solicitor will ask you to make a payment to cover their initial costs. This is usually about £1,000 but depends on the transaction size.

If you want to look at the full process, the Read Cooper Solicitors website explains it well. Follow this link: http://readcooper.com/residential.htm.

Before the exchange, your solicitor will send you a report on title. Read this. It's important. Your solicitor should also call you to go over any potential issues and make sure you understand the implications. Don't feel you can't pull out now just because you've spent some money. If there are issues that can't be overcome, walk away. It's better to lose the legal fees now than to lose even more later.

Look out for covenants. These restrict the use of a building or site. If your solicitor flags one, it's worth looking at because it can limit the value you can add to the property.

For example, Avi and I conditionally exchanged contracts on a large Victorian house on Amhurst Road in Hackney, in January 2016. It was a probate purchase. Once again, about a dozen siblings were arguing over the will. The conditions of the exchange were based on the probate being lifted but not the covenant.

Hackney Council had placed a covenant on the property in 1988 to say that it must remain a family home. But it was almost 3,000 square feet and there wasn't much demand for a property of that size in the area. It was more profitable for us to split it into flats.

We applied for planning permission to split the house and this was granted. But we still had the issue of the covenant. Based on legislation, once you have planning permission you should be able to apply for a court order to have the covenant lifted, but that was going to take time and we needed it quickly so we could raise the debt with our bank. After weeks of negotiation between our litigation solicitor and the council's solicitor we agreed to a one-off payment to reflect the additional profit we would make from splitting the titles. We were happy with that.

Over a year after the exchange, we're still no closer to completing. The siblings are still locked in litigation. Luckily, property prices are still going up in Hackney so we're benefitting from the increase. We locked in the price at December 2015 levels when we first had our offer accepted.

Review the local searches and check that there are no planning problems, rejected applications or other issues. Your solicitor will report these to you.

Until you have exchanged, either party can still pull out. There are companies that will lock in the sale if you buy a contract however I have not yet worked with them.

# Planning Permission

If you've bought a project with planning permission in place and you're comfortable that it makes the most of the building's potential, skip ahead to construction. If you don't have planning permission, don't start any work.

For me, planning permission is the second most frustrating part of the development process. There's just no consistency between boroughs or even between streets.

For example, at one of my properties the neighbours on either side had big extensions on their basements and their ground and first floors. The local council was adamant that we were only allowed to do a three-metre full-width extension on the basement and half width at ground level. This looked dwarfed by the five-and-a-half-metre extensions on either side. The council's response is always that past planning policy doesn't determine current planning policy.

## Working with an Architect

To get the planning process started you'll need to find an architect. Ask friends and neighbours. It can help if an architect is already known (in a good light, of course) to the planners, but it isn't essential. If in doubt, you might want to employ a planning consultant too.

Most importantly, find someone you believe you can work with for months, through ups and downs, while staying open and communicative. Like with a joint venture partner, it's not worth working with someone you don't like. As a developer herself, my architect Amrita understands where I'm coming from and I'm always open with her throughout the process.

Find an architect who understands that this is a commercial relationship. It's not about the architect's artistic licence unless they can show that their design is cost-effective or will bring you a return on your investment.

I also like to negotiate a number of site visits (at least once a fortnight) in my contract, as hourly fees are expensive. It's better to include this and pay upfront than be hit with a surprise bill at the end.

You could also consider working in a joint venture with your architect. Yes, really. With one project we agreed that if our architect lowered her fees by £2,000 we would give her a £7,000 bonus if the property sold for over a certain amount. I'm sure she was sceptical, but in the end she comfortably got her bonus.

Once you've negotiated (always negotiate) and agreed fees and terms, get your planning application in as quickly as possible. I like to negotiate as long a completion time as possible with the vendor so I have enough time to get the planning application in and the finance in place before we complete. This way, as soon as we complete I can hit the ground running.

## Working with Consultants

A good architect can submit a planning application on a straightforward scheme in a couple of weeks. Something more complex will take longer and often involves more consultants. Local authority planners will often insist you use these consultants.

The list of consultants is long, but the most common include:

- **PLANNING CONSULTANT** If you're not sure whether your planning application will be accepted, a planning consultant will help tighten your argument. They'll point out potential flaws and find legislation that supports your application. For the time you might lose if your application is refused it's worth the additional couple of thousand pounds in fees.

- **SURVEYOR** A surveyor will carry out a survey to verify the dimensions of a site and building. It's worth spending the £1,500 or so to get the measurements right.

- **ENVIRONMENTAL CONSULTANT** Environmental consultants cover many different areas. The most common, in my experience, are daylight and sunlight, the right to light and the impact of noise. Using an environmental consultant adds a couple of thousand pounds to your planning bill.

- **VIABILITY CONSULTANT** A viability consultant will assess whether or not your project makes sense financially and write up their findings in a report to support your application. For example, Avi and I are developing a property in an employment conservation area (an area the local authority prioritises employment over residential development). The local council is concerned that we are not providing enough space for employment, so we need to show we are doubling the current employment size. The quotes we're getting so far are around £4,000.

- **HERITAGE CONSULTANT** These specialist consultants advise on listed buildings and the policies surrounding them.

- **S.106 CONSULTANT** These consultants provide mathematical support for a lower s.106 contribution as part of your application. They'll negotiate this with the council on your behalf. The cost is £2,000 or more depending on the size of your scheme. (A section 106 agreement is a private agreement made between the developer and the local authority which sets out the private agreements and obligations assigned to the planning permission. Often, they include compensation to the local authority for affordable housing.)

Other consultants deal with flood assessments, leasehold extensions, contamination and many other issues. If the planners request it, there will be a consultant who you can pay to support your argument.

## Working with the Local Authority

It's worth brushing up on your basic permitted development rights (that is, what you can do with a property without planning permission) for when you're appraising a property. You can find them all on the Planning Portal.[12] They've got a good interactive tool for assessing what you can and can't do with a residential property. It will help with your decision on returns.

Be aware of conservation areas. If your property is in a conservation area, it can limit what you're allowed to build. For example, in City Road, where I have a rooftop development, a little block that includes the Moorfields Eye Hospital is a conservation area but the rest of the road isn't. This means we can't add more than two levels to the building.

Local authorities must respond to 60% of planning applications within eight weeks of submission and verification. It makes sense that planners seek out the straightforward 60% and process them while the rest wait. Shockingly, some are automatically rejected because planners don't have the resources to process them. I don't blame the planners: it's a thankless job and there are staff shortages. It's the system.

Local authorities encourage pre-apps because this notifies the council of what's being discussed rather than surprising them when you send the application. Based on personal experience, I'm not convinced of their worth. I find they're ambiguous at best and give little of value that you can't learn from a

---

12  https://www.planningportal.co.uk/info/200187/your
_responsibilities/37/planning_permission/2.

rejected application or continued dialogue. In my experience, the time frame is the same: eight weeks to receive a rejection, two weeks to reapply based on the notes and another eight weeks for a response. In my experience with pre-apps there's no time frame for a response so it can drag on.

## Planning Strategies

There's a great planning strategy that I use regularly: phased planning. Instead of submitting the full extent of the planning for a property, you break it into more palatable chunks for the planners. This means they're not overwhelmed by the complexity of an application. They can look at it bit by bit on its individual merits.

Paintworks is a lovely building on Kingsland Road near Hoxton Station. Avi and I secured it as a joint venture with other developers in summer 2016. The other developers brought the building to us because it was too big for them at the time.

The major attraction of the building was the large car park at the back. The council wants to reduce the use of cars, so schemes that reduce parking tend to appeal to them. We could see that by building over the car park we could more than triple the size of the building. If we sent an application that included building up, out and down as well as changed the commercial use it would be too much. So, we took a phased approach.

Phase one was extending the basement and ground floor over the carpark. By doing so, we could soon look for a tenant, which would help our valuation and bank finance. Phase two was building out over the extended areas on the first and second floors to provide more residential accommodation. Finally, phase three is building up another two storeys at around two-thirds and one-third of the size of the floors below, creating more valuable residential space. At the time of writing, we are waiting for a decision on phase two.

Another strategy is parallel applications. Like phased planning, this gives you options and saves time. Some might argue that you're giving the planners options and they'll approve the option with the least value to the developer; my experience is to the contrary.

I did my first parallel application on Parkholme Road. The original building was L-shaped at the back. I wanted to extend by three metres from the furthermost point and fill in all of the set-back section or at least go out three metres from the wall. Our architect suggested that we submit two applications and see what the planners decided.

To our delight, they approved the most valuable option: we

could extend the infill and the outer section all the way to form a straight line. I was surprised, as I was concerned that it would interfere with the neighbours' right to light. The neighbours opposed the application but we were able to settle our differences by building a new brick wall to replace a rickety timber one and including some new plants.

## Working with Tenants

Never underestimate the power of working with your current tenants for planning, especially a charitable organisation that has been there for a long time. It's essentially another form of joint venture, just with your tenants.

I'm working with two such tenants. The first is in Clapton. A church has been in this unattractive brick building for nearly twenty-five years and couldn't act quickly enough to make the purchase.

Our team is planning to build over the current car park in a scheme that features three separate buildings with mixed residential and commercial spaces. We've offered the church a sub-basement with large light wells and more useable space than they have at the moment. We hope they'll stay with us.

The other charity I'm working with is a youth charity in Hackney. We bought the building in January 2016. The property was marketed as vacant possession, but it has been the home of the youth club for forty-nine years. As a local, I didn't want to evict a long-standing charity.

We worked hard to keep the charity there. We put a tripartite agreement in place between us, the seller and the charity to make sure they could continue to occupy the new building.

We plan to build out the basement area for them, including the sports facilities they need to continue their good work with local young people. We're hoping a local school will take the ground floor and assist the charity by sub-letting their sporting facilities. The first, second and third levels will be residential.

Be warned: charities work at a different speed from you and I. Often they're run by volunteers, who have other jobs to do. Decisions are usually made by committee and it takes a while to get everyone in the same room.

It's worth persisting. Planners appreciate the effort you're making to continue to accommodate a long-standing charity. What I wasn't prepared for was a little kickback from some lenders. Some don't want to lend with a charity in place and risk retaliation if they have to evict them. But there are plenty of lenders who will lend.

# Construction

## In-House Building Teams

At the beginning of my property journey I decided that it made sense to keep my builders in-house. This meant I was fully in control of the process and budget. I didn't have to worry about adding a main contractor profit. I could be in charge of the schedule. Avi also took this approach (by accident), as outlined previously.

It's a lot of responsibility to take on tradespeople like this. You are in control of all health and safety on site, and you're ultimately responsible if things go wrong. I'm not going to go into this in detail in this book, but please review the laws and make sure your builder is compliant. You could be charged with manslaughter if things go wrong. The risks are too great not to do everything correctly.

## Budgeting

Budgeting for the construction is so important, yet it's so difficult to get right. It's an art rather than a science. By using accounting software you'll be able to refine your costs on a line-by-line basis, providing more accurate information for future projects. In the beginning, you have to do a certain extent of guessing.

You might be thinking, 'There are quantity surveyors!' Yes, there are, but it's supposed to be a mathematical process – five doors at £200 each, for example. That doesn't take into account time and materials overrunning or unforeseeable issues arising on site. Even a 10% contingency can't take into account every outcome.

Be aware that issues do arise and costs do overrun. Try to cut costs in other areas to offset the budget overspend. Sometimes this is impossible and you just need to go with it. Treat it as a learning experience and try to get the costs closer to the budget next time.

## Party Walls (Dealing with Neighbours)

I quickly learned how difficult neighbours can be. If you're trying to improve a property and increase the value of other properties on the street, you'd think that people might be patient with a few months of disruption. But in my experience this is rarely the case. On one property, the neighbour on one side was fantastic and I enjoyed him popping over for a regular nosey and a chat. (In fact, we went on to renovate his house for him.) But the neighbours on the other side were not so accommodating. At first, they tried to block our every move.

We had another funny experience with another development. Our party-wall surveyor had taken photos of the neighbour's garden in summer when it was looking its best. We started work and had to disrupt their garden to a certain extent to build a new brick wall to replace the timber fence, which was falling down. At the end, we reassembled their shed as agreed and put all their pots back in their former positions.

A couple of weeks later we received a sternly worded email from the neighbour's party-wall surveyor. It stated that we had not returned the garden to the condition that it was in as set out in our party-wall agreement. Enclosed in the letter was a picture of an RHS Chelsea Garden Show prize-winning garden. I couldn't stop laughing as I called my party-wall surveyor and showed him the pictures. We compared the before and after photos and agreed that we had met all requirements and it was a different garden in their pictures.

It's important to get the party-wall agreements in place as soon as possible. Legally, you're not supposed to start work without signed agreements in place. I try to save time by doing work that doesn't involve the party walls. There are deadlines that have to be met by law, but making the agreement can drag on for months. It's worth getting a proactive party-wall surveyor and hoping that the neighbours do the same. Remember, you have to pay their costs.

You can also do it yourself. It can be much easier to go down this route. I did this with Parkholme Road. The architect and I went to see the neighbours one Saturday morning. We had the plans and walked through the way the works would affect them. As compensation for the disruption I agreed to repoint their external brickwork, repaint all internal walls along the party wall and build a new brick wall to their requirements. We then drew up a simple contract outlining the expectations of both parties, took photos of how it looked before, and signed the photos and the contract.

## New Home Warranties

If you're doing title split, converting a house into flats or selling any multiple-dwelling development, you'll be asked during the sales conveyancing process for a ten-year building warranty. I wasn't prepared with Graham Road so I didn't start the process until near the end of the build. Ideally you should start this process before you've even started the work on site. Get it arranged early.

I called one company and after answering a few questions I was given a quote of £80,000. Yes, that's right. I was in shock. I rang a developer friend in a panic. She recommended a couple of other companies, one of which quoted me a much more realistic price at around £5,000. What a difference!

In my experience, the company sends their own surveyor to monitor the progress on site. At the end, if all goes well, they will issue you with the new building warranty for ten years.

## Utilities

Another thing to consider early is any water, gas and electricity connections. Be prepared for this to take months and to deal with problems caused by high staff turnover. (In my experience, every time someone leaves you start all over again and are given a new set of requirements.) You'll need the patience of a saint. If you haven't got that, outsource it to your project manager to protect your heart health.

## Project Management Software

Whether you're managing the build yourself or outsourcing it, having an efficient way to manage the various stages is a must. Google Drive or Dropbox are essential for sharing documents. I prefer Google Drive because it's so simple.

For each project, I set up a separate folder. I then have eight separate numbered folders as follows:

- Purchase
- Finance
- Planning
- Construction
- Utilities
- Sales
- Lettings
- Photos

These are self-explanatory and follow the processes I've set out in this book. I store every document I receive by email in these folders. This means they're always available from my phone or in the cloud, no matter where I am. My team all have access to the folders, as do the investors in the project. I'm completely transparent and they have access to everything.

When we're having a valuation, I can invite the valuer to share the finance folder so they can access all the information they need. The same goes for the broker, the many surveyors, the construction team and all the parties involved.

My drives are sacred – everyone knows not to mess with them. They're constantly in use and I rely on them to contain all the available information. My business is now completely on my phone and shareable remotely.

I have a love/hate relationship with email. I get a lot of it. I try to stay on top of it, but it's difficult. I really dislike emails that just say 'Thank you' or that someone is going to do a task I have asked them to do. Thank you is implicit, and I'd rather someone emails me when a task is done. For this reason, I've started to use task management systems.

A task management system like Asana or Basecamp allows you to separate all communication by project. If your architect needs to communicate about an issue, rather than send an email they can send a message in Basecamp. All communication is then in one place. You don't have to search through email. You can assign tasks to your team to make sure everyone is hitting their deadlines. It makes it easier to oversee the whole project when all the files and photos are in one spot. It's so much better than having hundreds of emails flying around the ether.

Better still, find a tasking system that speaks to your accounting software and add your investors so they can see what's going on with their project.

## CIS and VAT

I'm not going into much detail about the Construction Industry Scheme (CIS) or value added tax (VAT). Do an online search for basic information and speak to your accountant about how these taxes affect you.

CIS is something that you (if you've got an in-house construction team) or the main contractor must pay. It's 20% of subcontractors' salary. In practice, my guys would say they wanted to earn £100 a day so I'd have to pay them £120 a day. It really adds up, so budget for it.

Some people say they have ways of working around CIS. But from discussions with my accountant none of these are legal and you just have to pay. A main contractor will factor it into their invoice so you won't ever see it as an item on the bill.

VAT is another tax you'll have to pay. You can't add VAT to the price of a residential property so you can't claim it back. The only exception is if you're buying a commercial property that is VAT-rated. You'll then need to register for VAT and claim it back on the purchase price.

Some properties, such as listed buildings or buildings being converted from a house into flats, have reduced VAT at 5%. The reduced rating applies only to the supply and installation of fixtures and fittings. In these situations, you can't claim back the VAT but you have to self-certify to the supplier when you buy the fixtures and fittings. For example, if you're having a kitchen fitted in a listed building, you need to tell the supplier when you buy the kitchen that you're eligible for a reduced rate. The supplier needs to adjust the invoice. If you've already paid their full invoice you can't claim back the difference between the 20% and reduced rate, so be sure from the beginning.

See the Gov.UK website for more information: https://www .gov.uk/vat-builders/houses-flats

## Building Control and Fire Regulations

Before you start on site you must appoint a building regulations company. Local authorities also have building control officers. The local authority has the last say, so if you disagree with your building regulations company you can apply to the local authority's building regulations department and they can rule. But if you're only using the local authority there's no recourse if you disagree.

While I've generally had good experiences, unexpected problems do come up. For example, just as we were near the end of the title split, our building regulations inspector told us we might need to install an automatic opening valve system for fire regulations. We had already closed all the walls and had started decorating. We got a quote for around £30,000 to design and install the system, and it cost us £5,000 just to get the quote.

I read up on the fire regulations and decided that the inspector was wrong. A discussion with a fire regulations expert confirmed my view. I paid yet another consultant £5,000 to produce a report setting out why we didn't need an opening valve system. I sent this to the head of building control. He said he would review it but he couldn't promise anything because we'd already had a decision from a senior inspector.

Week after nail-biting week passed with no answer from the council. If they ruled that we needed the system it was going to cost tens of thousands of pounds. It would also cost me the sales of the three flats – they had exchanged conditionally with a long-stop date of September 2016. There was no way we could finish the installation and repair the damage by then.

After a month had passed, I called the manager. He asked for a site meeting. At the meeting, they inspected the finished flats. The inspectors said they were the best examples of flat conversions they'd seen. Rather humorously, they asked if they could submit our project into a London-wide inter-borough competition for best practice. I never found out if they won, but it was a vote of confidence in the developments we were producing.

What I learned from this is that it's important to stay in constant communications with your building regulations inspector. Never get too far ahead without an inspection or it could cost you time and money as you rip back your work to expose the items they need to inspect.

## Getting Started

Now that everything is in place, it's time to start the heavy lifting. You and your builder should have sat down and decided on the order of works. You should have identified whether the builder or project manager is ordering the fixtures, fittings and other materials when they're needed, taking note of lead times. Some kitchens, windows, doors and flooring systems can take weeks. I once ordered some sliding glass doors that took twenty weeks to arrive. This pushed back the whole schedule by sixteen weeks. That's a long time when you're trying to make a profit.

This is one area where it pays to have an experienced builder and project manager on site to keep the project on schedule. They'll pay for themselves in time and budget savings.

I really enjoyed working with my builder, for many reasons. One reason is that he loves to find a bargain. I'd send him the shower mixer I wanted, for example, and within thirty minutes he'd found the same one for much less. I once needed a lift to help install some steel beams. He worked out that we could buy the lift for less than the cost of hiring it, and then we'd always have it.

If you're renovating a house, ask yourself whether you can patch up what's there or whether you need to strip right back to the brick. In the beginning, I would patch up what was there, replacing things as needed. But I found that I never got the crisp finish I wanted. It wasn't until Englefield Road, where I stripped everything back to three walls and no roof, that I saw the difference in finish. The relatively small price difference justified the better finish I got by stripping everything out.

## Interiors: Lighting, Plumbing and Everything Else Inside

While my guys are busy with the stripping-out and demolition phase, I turn my attention to the interiors.

I cannot stress enough how important it is to have full interiors plans drawn up early in the process. They should tell you where every shower, toilet, light, socket and switch is going to be. This avoids second-guessing where to put things, which allows the project to continue with speed.

I love interiors and I believe I have a good eye. But superior interior design takes time. Going through various boards on Pinterest to refine how you want each room to look is a skill that I thought I had until I started. It wasn't long before I outsourced it to Amrita, my architect.

Having an architect who is also an interior designer is so efficient. Amrita can design in a holistic way, incorporating all the features – inside and out.

Even if you're working with an interior designer, consider using Pinterest or Houzz boards to give your designer an idea of the direction you're heading in and your taste. It saves them time guessing and gives them direction. Like your architect, your interior designer should be able to listen to your requirements and budget the design accordingly.

In my own home, I overlooked the importance of lighting. I dislike spotlights so I refused to have any in my house. This means I have to live with only a single, or sometimes two, pendants in each large room. It's frustratingly dark in some rooms. One day I'll have it fixed, but my team are all so busy…

I've worked with a great lighting designer who doesn't charge a fee on his design – instead, he takes a commission on the lighting. It's a brilliant service. He'll work with the architect and interior designer to make sure they're happy with what he recommends. It's worth the extra money to have it done correctly.

At this stage, it's also important to consider installing audio-visual systems and future-proofing your developments. I install CAT 5 (cabling for computer networks) systems as a minimum, and always where TVs and audio equipment might be. Try to make sure the house will support new developments in technology. You can call on specialists for these services. Just make sure you plan for as much as possible.

# Sales

## Off-Plan Sales

The time to think about selling is before you've even started the construction. As soon as you get your planning application back and you know what you've got to sell, start selling. Known as off-plan sales, it allows you to sell a property before you have completed the construction or even before you have started.

I didn't realise that off-plan sales were available to smaller developers like me. I thought it was just for the big companies like Berkeley Homes and Galliard. But many agents have whole departments for new home sales. For Graham Road, I decided to have a go at selling off-plan. My agent really earned their commission. Despite my best intentions to be organised and prepared for the sale, things didn't go quite to plan.

The first step is to finalise the interiors and the specification list. These finishes are what sell the property. Then have your interior designer or architect work with a computer-generated image specialist to perfect the renders. Be realistic. Don't put in crystal chandeliers if you intend to use IKEA lighting. Make sure the specification list is realistic. You have to deliver on this – it's contractual.

These computer-generated images and specification lists go to the agent along with the floorplans. The agent uses them to produce their sales particulars. You then approve them and the property goes live. The agent will need to carry out viewings with potential buyers, so ensure your site is safe at all times and looking as good as it can, considering it's a building site. Foxtons put up large, catchy sales boards on the hoarding. Don't forget to put up your own boards – it's the perfect opportunity for brand-building. Everyone's curious about a building site. Get your name in view.

Once you get an acceptable offer the agent will have the buyer sign an agreement and put down a non-refundable deposit generally around £2,000. This is to secure the property and is taken off the exchange deposit.

The conveyancing process is much the same as with an ordinary property, except that there is no fixed completion date. There is an indicative date for mortgage purposes and a long-stop date. As the developer, you need to be mindful of this long-stop date because if you can't deliver by then the buyer can pull out, taking their full deposit. It's important to have this in the contract for the buyer because their mortgage has an expiry date. They will need to reapply if you go over that date.

What's so great about selling off-plan is that once you've completed the project, you've completed the sale. The funds, and hopefully a profit, are banked immediately. There's no marketing period.

A potential downside to selling off-plan is that you might give away a little profit by not having your beautifully finished product on display. This is especially true if your finished product specification is high. But to me, the benefit of booking the profit outweighs the loss of further profit.

# Traditional Sale

Most people go down the traditional sales route. There's nothing new I can tell you here except that there are more and more online agents. You might consider using one. Your decision depends on how much time you have to package up the property and run the viewings. I prefer to outsource this to an agent and pay them the commission.

My view is that an agent's commission isn't earned doing the viewings; it's pushing the sale through to exchange. That's the true value of an agent and it shouldn't be underestimated. Many a good agent has turned around a sale that was on the brink of collapsing. A long chain on one property would have broken on several occasions if it hadn't been for the skill and patience of the agents.

I've recently toyed with the idea of bringing sales in-house. This would give me full control over the sales process and save on commission costs. This person or team could also help with sourcing properties and sorting through the dozens of properties sent to me every week. With a Rightmove subscription and good relationships with traditional agents, there's no reason why we can't do a lot more ourselves. It makes even more sense if you're selling larger developments flat by flat and off-plan.

Galliard Homes do this really well. They're actually a marketing company first and a home-builder second. I believe this should be the goal of all companies. How many other developers can have people camping overnight to secure a fully priced flat in Canary Wharf? Only Galliard. A few miles west at the Nine Elms development it's an entirely different story. Branding and marketing is everything.

# Staging

Staging is the one thing you should always do, regardless of how you sell. Even if it's your own home you're selling, strip out the junk. Make it look like a magazine. No one needs to see pictures of your kids on the beach or your shopping lists on the fridge. It isn't hard – get some moving boxes, pack away all your superfluous items and put them in storage.

If you're trying to sell a property after it's been rented and it's looking tired, spend a few hundred quid. Get the painters in. Fresh paint makes more difference than the price you pay for it. Under no circumstances should you paint the walls magnolia. Never! White or a hint of grey is best.

For staging, pick some basic but stylish furniture to fill the main rooms – kitchen, dining room, living room and master bedroom. It's fine to leave the other rooms empty. The exception is if one bedroom is very small. You might want to put a single bed in to show that it's large enough.

I rent a garage and keep some basics ready for staging. These include a good sofa, a side chair, a coffee table, a rug, a side table, a TV, a dining table and chairs, a king-sized bed, bedside tables and a larger side chair. Don't forget all the soft furnishings. You'll need a couple of rugs and throws, some cushions, art, some books, a full dinner set to put on the table, and towels and branded soaps in the bathrooms. A tip I picked up from Amrita is to put some flowers in vases. If you can't go every few days to water a plant or change flowers, use dried flowers. They can look just as effective.

Some carefully placed books, magazines and other props make a big difference. I like to put a retro coffee machine in the kitchen with some nice mugs to make the property feel warm. Browse through Pinterest and find a style that's classic but classy, which will work in any property. Then spend £2,000 to £5,000 on that staging kit. It will pay for itself after the first sale. Sometimes the buyer wants to buy everything, including the furniture – give it to them if it means the sale goes through. It's a sweetener. And you can then have the fun of buying something fresher for the next project.

# Forward sales

A new concept for me is that of forward selling a whole building. It first came about with our development on Midland Road in Luton. Following a post I made on LinkedIn showing the vacant site, an agent contacted me and asked if we would be interested in selling it. I created a small sales brochure and we ended up with a mini bidding war and an offer of £1 million more than we expected (we subsequently decided not to sell it).

With a forward sale, you still construct or develop the project; you just lock in a sale at the beginning of the project. It's expected that you'll sell at a discount in exchange for the risk they're taking in buying an unbuilt property. Think of it as an off-plan sale except the buyer is purchasing the whole building before it has been constructed.

The process is similar to selling a single flat off-plan. You create a sales pack with the floorplans, computer-generated images and specification list. You take a 10% deposit at exchange and there's a long-stop date for the completion.

It's a great way to lock in a sale. The profit is then yours to lose based on your ability to stick to the budget. If you go over budget, it comes out of your pocket and there's no way of earning it back.

## Plan B

Life doesn't always go to plan, and neither do property sales. You need a plan B. My plan B is always to rent out the property on a short-term basis until a sale is agreed. If you're short-letting a property while selling, make sure the tenant is aware of this from the start. You might want to offer them a slight discount for the inconvenience. Agree to a set number of viewings a week with a twenty-four hours' notice and stick to it. Keep the tenant happy. They might only be short term but you never know, they might want to buy the property.

# Summary

- Decide on what property strategy suits you best based on your time commitments, cash available or access to capital, and your existing skills.

- Ensure that you work with the right professionals, accountant and solicitors to make sure that the investment structure is correct for your chosen strategy.

- Get started: purchase your first property. First choose an area, specify a property type and then appraise as many deals as you can until you find one that meets your criteria. Then just do it.

- Become familiar with what you can and can't do without planning permission. Also, find a good architect and perhaps planning consultant to advise you.

- Ask around and find the right builder or construction team for your project. It helps to be organised from the beginning and find someone you can work closely with for a long time. You must feel like you can trust your team.

- Identify an exit strategy. You should do this along with selecting a strategy and identifying a first project. Be sure you know what the end goal will be before you undertake the works. A buy-to-sell strategy will have a different structure but also a different finish to a luxury buy-to-sell project. Be clear and work towards that goal.

- Be flexible. If things don't turn out as expected have a backup plan. Speak to your professionals about the Plan B from the beginning so that the structure can be amended for the circumstances.

# Getting Started

## Take the First Steps

You might be tempted to book yourself on a course to get started. Property education isn't regulated, and it attracts some people who make a profit from courses rather than property. There are some good sources of education and information: try Property Tribes and Property Fortress. Some of the Facebook property groups can be good, but be cautious – they're open to all.

If I were starting again, I would do so in the following order:

- **BRAND** Come up with a brand name. It could be your surname, a heritage name like East Eight or something completely unrelated. Register the website and all the social media handles. Even if you register the brand name, consider using your own name on Twitter, Instagram and Snapchat to make it personal. Ask your accountant or solicitor to register the company name too, as this makes it scalable. This doesn't have to be the same name as the brand, but it can be useful if it is.

- **STRATEGY** Draw up your property strategy based on your cash flow requirements and time available – now and in the future. Set out how it's going to look, feel and operate. Include staffing requirements. Set goals for the next two, six and twelve months. Think about the longer term too.

- **STRUCTURE** Speak with your accountant to ensure that your company is structured in the right way. They will make sure you're investing in the most tax-effective and compliant way. Consider loan agreements if you're lending your company the starting capital. Also consider how much income you'll draw from the company, when you will take it and how – dividends, income, et cetera. Discuss employees as well. Outsourcing is cheapest, but it might not be best for your business. Find a good book-keeper to stay on top of your books throughout your project.

- **FINANCE** Find a good broker and get an idea of how much money you can borrow and how. Your broker should do a full review of your situation and advise you on the best way forward.

- **CONVEYANCING SOLICITOR** Ask friends and contacts for a good conveyancing solicitor. A conveyancing solicitor should be quick and able to focus on your transaction while still being thorough. It's good to have a conveyancing solicitor in place before you find a property so you already have a relationship when you're ready to buy.

- **PROPERTY** Find a property! This is the exciting part. You know how much money you have to spend on the purchase and the works. Go shopping. Speak to local agents, walk the streets, get to know your chosen patch. Once you find the right property, make an offer. What's the worst that can happen? Don't get carried away, though – stick to your budget.

- **ARCHITECTS AND PROJECT MANAGERS** If you're going down this route, ask friends and contacts for recommendations. Ask to see their previous projects and ask plenty of questions about keeping to budgets and timescales. The hardest part is finding an architect who can be commercially-minded for developers. Most are geared towards owner-occupiers who are not so price sensitive. The same advice goes for project managers. Your architect can also project-manage to some extent or provide a trusted contact.

- **BUDGET** Budgeting for a build is an art, not a science. There are so many variables that even quantity surveyors get it wrong. Your architect or project manager should be able to advise you on your budget for each item. Once you've had more experience you can look back at your accounts to see where you're going over and under the budget. This will help for future developments.

- **BUILDERS** Ask friends or other developers to recommend good builders. What you need depends on the extent of the works and your budget. Get three or four quotes. If the builder takes too long to get back to you, take this as a sign that they're overworked and can't commit to your job. If it's a large project, ask to see their previous projects. Hopefully, they'll have good relationships with past clients and will be happy to show you. Your architect will arrange the tender process if you're using them for this service. Of course, you can always do this work yourself.

Now you should be ready to get the project underway. The rest is up to you to oversee and keep on track. After that, the next step is to either sell or rent. The agent you bought through might be the best place to start. You can also consider the options we covered in Chapter Four.

If all this sounds too daunting and you need a helping hand, you can always invest in one of our crowdfunding raises. We'll be running special Invest to Learn programmes so you can, as the name suggests, learn while you're investing and piggyback off our knowledge and contacts.

# Outsourcing

During the Q&A at my first speaking engagement at the Women in Property and Business Network, a lady raised her hand. She asked me 'So you raise three kids nearly singlehanded, run a house, stay fit and run a business with a dozen builders? What are you, Superwoman?' The tone of the question was slightly facetious, but I ignored that while I pondered the question. 'Of course not,' I replied. 'I outsource.'

After I'd had my third child and I was trying to balance looking after three kids aged three and under as a solo parent (look on Google) with my home refurbishment, I realised I needed to learn to outsource. It didn't come naturally to me. I took it as a sign of weakness that I couldn't do it all. It just wasn't the

Australian thing to have anything more than a weekly house-keeper. As I saw the benefits, I started to outsource more.

At the time when I was asked that question I had a cook, a part-time nanny/housekeeper and a part-time personal assistant and bookkeeper. If you think a cook costs a fortune, think again. For £60 a week, a lovely professional cook came to my house and prepared as much food as she could in four hours. It was heaven. Sadly, it didn't last. Travelling from Luton to Hackney was too much for her. But we've since found an equally talented replacement.

It wasn't until I took on a full-time member of staff that I could really grow my business. Before that I didn't have the bandwidth to take on any more work. I did marketing and social media on an ad hoc basis whenever I had time, I juggled managing the various projects and, I confess, on a couple of projects I really did take my eye of the ball. Costs overran and I don't think the build team were as efficient as they could have been.

As soon as I took on a full-time employee I could outsource all the marketing and project oversight to her. This let me focus on finding new projects and investors and structuring the debt and equity finance – this was the best use of my time.

I'd recommend finding a bookkeeper. Even if your business is quite straightforward, it's highly beneficial to have the books in order and ready for your accountant when the accounts are due. Most importantly, they can give you a quick snapshot of where you are in relation to your budget at any time.

Have your bookkeeper set up the accounts in the way that works best for you so you can see the information you need to see. For example, when I see the accounts on each project I want to see the total spend, which includes the purchase price and those related costs. I also want to see just the build and professional fees that relate direct to the build costs. This helps me keep a tight rein on these costs and see how I'm getting on with the budget.

As mentioned previously, accurate line items will help you prepare budgets for future projects. This will help you appraise projects before you buy. It will also help you prepare the valuation spreadsheets for the bank (for lending) and for investors (for equity).

Remember, no one has the same vision as you do, but there are many people who are better at running the various parts of the business. Let them do it. It's that old adage: there are many ways to skin a cat. Just because someone isn't doing things your way doesn't mean it's the wrong way. Don't micro-manage all the time: sometimes let people make their own way. It empowers them.

# Emotional Ups and Downs of Property

During the planning process for this book I posted my notes on Instagram and asked for feedback. Someone asked me to write about the emotional ups and downs of the property business. I had completely overlooked the emotional side. Yet it's almost impossible to talk about business without considering the emotions.

I think the property journey is a bit like childbirth: if you remembered in detail the emotional rollercoaster you went on, you wouldn't do it again. Or perhaps it's what separates those who are suited to this career from those who are not. Many people renovate a property once and never want to do it again. It is difficult; I won't sugar-coat it. Things don't go to plan and you need to rely on so many external parties that it's hard to keep things to a schedule.

By looking at the process of buying a property you can track the stressor points. First you have the euphoria of finding the perfect property. Then there's the stress over your offer – will they or won't they accept? Are you up against others? You get the property and the euphoria hits again. Then there are the next steps.

Conveyancing can be particularly stressful. How stressful it is depends on your solicitor, the vendor's solicitor and the motivation of all parties, including the agent. If everyone is motivated and there are no hidden agendas, things can go relatively smoothly. That is, until the council fails to send through the searches on time or an old planning issue is thrown up.

Valuations are the most stressful part for me. These usually coincide with the exchange, which is a huge high – you have secured the property. Then, oh dear, you have a set number of weeks to secure the debt and equity. I hope you never have to go to exchange without having the funds to complete, but sometimes you have no choice.

Banks take their sweet time arranging debt finance. It frustrates me how slow they are. But the flip side is that they're cheap. If you want speed, you pay for it – 6% to 24% a year from a bridging lender versus 3.25% or thereabouts for a high street bank. If it's a quick completion you have no choice. Then there's the dreaded valuation. So often the valuers mark down the value of the property, meaning you have to dip your hand back into your pocket for the equity if you want to complete.

Completion is a big high: you've paid for the property and you're full of optimism. We all hope the construction process is smooth, but things can get thrown up, as they often do, causing emotional lows. Budgets and going over them can be especially painful, especially if you have to explain it to investors.

Once you're finished, you need to find a tenant or a buyer. Both options can be problematic depending on the market. The sales conveyancing is a nail-biting experience as you wish the sale through to exchange. The added stress at this stage of the process is that often you're out of cash. You're desperate to get back the funds you've invested and realise the profit.

Since the market has quietened I've found that buyer drop-off at exchange is a problem. There's no urgency to complete and buyers aren't willing to compromise like they are in a rising market. My Mare Street property has had three buyers pull out at exchange. At the time of writing, I'm still waiting to sell. It's frustrating when the issue is not the pricing but something that has gone wrong for the buyer and their mortgage situation.

At the beginning of my journey my biggest problem was regular cash flow. I didn't quite have enough cash coming in at different times to give me the visibility and stability to hire my first full-time employee. Joint ventures were what solved this for me. Yes, I had to share the profits, but at least it gave me more certainty.

A word of caution – don't expect to achieve the same level of growth as I have experienced in such a short time. I was in the fortunate position to start with over £1 million of my own cash, find the ideal joint venture partner immediately and invest in the buoyant, rising market of London from 2012 to 2015. But if you invest with carefully chosen partners in solid investments you'll be well on your way to growing your pot of cash to invest.

Even with the cash, ideal market conditions and a good partner, success didn't just happen. It was hard work. I don't believe people who say they don't work hard and things just happen. It takes a significant amount of graft to get to that level. Since 2012 I have worked tirelessly on my business, taking just one winter holiday a year and the obligatory trips home to Australia. It wasn't until the summer of 2016 that I was able to take a few weeks off.

If I'm honest though, I had to take the time off. I was completely burned out. I looked at how good my investors had it while I worked my butt off and wished I was one of my investors instead. Years of hard work had taken its toll on my personal life. I wasn't happy with my workload and the sacrifices I'd made. I needed to take time to reassess what I wanted and where I was going. Thankfully, projects were winding down and I had Marina and Anna to help out. So, I checked out of my business and took the kids away so I could be the mother I wanted to be.

We went camping in France, to the beach in Italy and to the mountains of Austria. I also took advantage of grandparents so I could have a solo week off in an ashram high in the Austrian Alps, with dodgy reception and limited wi-fi. We practised four hours of meditation and four hours of yoga a day. We spent the rest of the time hiking in the mountains and swimming in freezing lakes.

I know it's a cliché, but this time out recharged and recentred me and reignited my hunger to succeed. I made a lot of changes in the strategy of the business after that summer, deciding to focus on fund management rather than construction. It was a big decision, given that I'd had my own construction team since 2012, but I felt it was the best way to focus my time. Avi had more experience in his construction team and they were more efficient as a result. It also meant the back-office operations for the construction would be his responsibility, not mine.

So far, this strategy has worked well. We raised £1.4 million in just nine days in November through crowdfunding with Simple Equity. A couple of weeks later we raised another £732,000 for another project. We're currently working on eleven projects across London worth over £120 million. Many of these are in construction with completion dates in early 2018. I've raised the cash and now I need to prove we can execute and build them out profitably.

From an initial target of one to two properties a year, I've built it up to a larger business with ambitions to expand it further.

I hope my summary of the process hasn't been too pessimistic. The property journey does have ups and downs. That's the nature of it. Try to take time off when you're having a down. Even if it's just switching off the phone for an afternoon and having a box set binge. This will recharge you and remind you of your purpose – why you decided to do this and what's driving you. Remember, this is not a get-rich-quick scheme. Property is damn hard work and you need to be prepared for that. If you can't stand the heat, as they say, stay out of that kitchen.

# Summary

- Just get started. Don't get bogged down in the planning stage for too long. Just make the first steps. Often the best lessons are learned while you're in the project.

- Outsource as much as possible as early as possible. Focus on the overall development of your business rather than the minutiae of the projects. Sometimes you do need to let go and let others take over. They might not do it your way but at least it is getting done leaving you free to focus on building the business for the longer term.

- It won't all be easy. Even with the best business plan and well-drafted strategy something will come up. At the risk of sounding wishy washy, do look at the big picture and work through the smaller issues. These issues are resolved and fade into distant memories.

# What Next?

I hope that by reading my story you've picked up some tips you can immediately apply to your own property journey. As I've said, I'm not an expert. I've tried some things that work and some that don't. Luckily, most of them have worked for me and I've scaled up quickly but carefully.

My journey has been an exciting one and thankfully I've blocked out most of the downs but managed to take on board the lessons the trials have taught me.

So, what's next? On the fundraising side, I'd like to beat the current highest crowdfund of £4.15 million raised in 2014. We're working on a number of potential projects for this. I also believe we can fill a project in minutes. For our second raise we lowered the minimum investment to £500 from £5,000. This allowed many more investors to access developments that are usually only available to larger investors. We have such a fantastic fan base waiting for our next development. What an exciting position to be in!

The feedback from many of our investors is that they want to learn how to invest and have full access to the project they've invested in. Later in 2017 we're launching our Invest to Learn programme, which allows our investors access to our projects.

Finally, we're hoping to build on the growth of our online community with a Facebook group and more engagement across the other platforms, especially Snapchat. I'm thoroughly enjoying this informal approach to engagement. Included in this is our foray into TV with our own YouTube property channel. I'm sure you'll agree that the next couple of years are guaranteed to be exciting.

We're also working on a secret project. It might involve a TV channel but we can't divulge too much. All I can say is watch this space.

I wish you all the best with your property journey. Do connect with me on social media so I can share in that journey. I will follow everyone who follows me. My handles are all below.

Twitter: @NicoleBremner
Snapchat: @nsbremner
Instagram: @nsbremner
Facebook: @NicoleSBremner

If you have any comments or suggestions or if you would like more tips, please follow us on the social media platforms of your choice. You can contact me at contact@east-eight.com. As I've said, I'm not an expert. I can only share my experience with you and hope you can pick up some tips from this.

I genuinely believe that the best way to learn is to just do something. To borrow a Chinese proverb 'Tell me and I'll forget; show me and I may remember; involve me and I'll understand'.

# ACKNOWLEDGEMENTS

The idea for this book was conceived in the summer of 2016. I was burned out by a tough few years of building my business. The summer of 2015 had been an emotional rollercoaster as I single-handedly tried to manage three young children on seven-and-a-half-weeks of school holiday while running a business solo.

Overburdened with work and guilt that I wasn't being the mother I wanted to be, I decided on a whim to take most of the summer of 2016 off. I booked a cabin by the beach near Cape Breton with some friends and their children and spent a lovely week relaxing by the pool and on the beach.

It was during this time that I discovered Nick Spalding. His books are so entertaining and, amazingly, he wrote some of them in just a couple of days. If he was able to expertly write a book so quickly I didn't see why I couldn't. I decided that planning was key.

I'd learned a bit about planning a book and the importance of writing a book from the Key Person of Influence course with Daniel Priestley in 2012. Taking that original guidance, I mapped out what my book might look like.

Luckily for me, one of my oldest and dearest friends is a professional writer. While I lay by the pool we exchanged WhatsApp messages about how to write a page-turner. James, I'm not sure if I've achieved this, but if not it's in no way a reflection of your tuition. Thank you.

I'd left my laptop in London so I couldn't start the book straight away. Some people can write before work or before the kids wake up. I couldn't do that. I wanted to plunge into it head first. I decided that Christmas and New Year 2016 would be my time. We take a family ski trip for three weeks then, so I'd have the time to focus without being interrupted by emails and calls.

Because of my fantastic planning, this book pretty much wrote itself in just thirteen days while I was skiing and looking after my endlessly hungry family. If you're planning your own book, I can vouch for this system. Thanks also goes to Joe Gregory and Lucy McCarraher at Rethink Press. Joe pushed me to finalise my cover when I was pushing back against my own self-doubt while Lucy painstakingly edited my text into something readable.

I'd like to say a special thank you to my team. Thanks to Anna Szyfer, who has worked with me since 2009. She's witnessed many of the changes in my path and has grown along with me. Marina Conway-Gordon, thank you for your patience. Starting in early 2016, Marina has allowed my business to grow into something I'd never envisaged. I appreciate having her there as a sounding board and sanity-checker. Jane Scroggs, who joined us late in 2016, has been invaluable in assisting with investor relations and general joviality.

I'm thankful for my business partner Avi's straight-talking approach to property and life in general. His thirty years in property has shaped my career and driven me to achieve more than I thought possible. Thanks also to Avi's team, especially Aga, for the continuous assistance 24/7/365.

Thanks to all the people I contacted to review my book. I appreciate the time you took to read a raw draft and give your honest feedback, guidance and insight.

To my kids – I love you, I'm proud of you and I'm doing this for you. I hope at least one of you will come and join me in the business one day.

I'd like to acknowledge and thank my grandparents for instilling strong values and a strong work ethic in me. As dairy farmers, you toiled from sunrise to sunset for years on end without a holiday. Pa, thanks for your patience as I followed you around the farm attempting to teach you how to systemise your business to make it more economically viable and efficient while I really knew little.

Thanks, Mum, for sacrificing so much for me and my brothers as we were growing up. It's only now that I'm a parent that I truly understand how much you did. I appreciate it all.

Thanks, Dad, for letting me assist you with the rivet gun many years ago and for being continually interested in the property industry.

A final thank you goes to my partner, Michael. We've been together for over seventeen years through many ups and downs, in various cities and through several career changes. During this time, while I've changed frequently you've always stayed the same. I appreciate your discipline and hard graft. No one works harder than you, as evidenced by your continual success. Thanks for letting me have my moment.

# THE AUTHOR

Originally from Australia, Nicole followed love and a dream to London,
where she now lives in Hackney with
her partner, Michael, and their two
sons and daughter. In what little free
time she has, Nicole enjoys running,
weight-lifting and yoga, as well as hiking and skiing.

In 2012, Nicole established East Eight as a development and
construction company. Soon after, she partnered with experienced property developer Avi Dodi and together they set
up a development company, London Central Developments.
By 2016, Nicole had refocused her business and East Eight
evolved to become the funds-management partner for London Central Developments. She remains active in all aspects

of the business – acquisition, purchase, construction, sales and funds management.

By May 2017, Nicole had raised over £4 million in crowdfunding with Simple Equity for four projects. More crowdfunding will follow in the coming months.

East Eight was the runner-up for the Property Investor Awards Property Development of the Year Award 2016. Working with architect and interior designer Amrita Mahindroo, their Englefield Road property was shortlisted for the International Design and Architecture Award for Living Space in 2015.

www.nicolebremner.com
www.east-eight.com
www.londoncentraldevelopments.com

Made in the USA
San Bernardino, CA
07 October 2017